Sexual Outsiders

Praise for *Sexual Outsiders*

"Written by a psychotherapist who specializes in kink-friendly sex therapy and a research psychologist, this book offers a nonjudgmental glimpse into the world of BDSM (Bondage/Discipline, Dominance/submission, Sadism/Masochism). In a supportive tone, David M. Ortmann and Richard A. Sprott discuss the way society misunderstands a potentially healthy set of sexual behaviors, employing largely Jungian analysis to explain the appeal of kinky play and including a generous selection of fascinating case studies drawn from Ortmann's private practice. The book provides encouragement for people who feel marginalized by their sexual preferences (and includes a guide to finding a sex therapist). The authors definitively dismiss popular claims that BDSM practitioners are mentally unwell or that their behaviors result from abusive childhoods. Instead, they describe the eroticism of power, the playacting of shame, and even show how this kind of play can serve as its own form of therapy. Ortmann and Sprott highlight the difference between the appearance of a behavior and its 'psychological meaning and impact.' The heart of the work is the individual stories of Ortmann's clients, chief among them the moving stories of BDSM practitioners 'coming out' as 'kinky' to the people in their lives." —***Publishers Weekly***

"This is the book I needed fifteen years ago when I started stumbling my way through treating the Kink community. It's answered all my questions. It should be mandatory reading for all ethical clinicians who should know something about treating alternative sexualities by now. The clinical community needs to stop retraumatizing, marginalizing, pathologizing, and trying to 'fix' the people who come to them for help. Either they need to learn the skills taught in this book or refer 'sexual outsiders' out to someone educated, trained, and willing to give these individuals the treatment they need and deserve. This book is for anyone who practices BDSM, treats patients struggling with related issues, and for anyone interested in further understanding this lifestyle and its community." —**Dorothy Hayden**, LCSW, Manhattan Center for Sex Addiction Therapy, Kink Aware psychotherapist, speaker, and author

"In *Sexual Outsiders*, authors David M. Ortmann and Richard A. Sprott perfectly complement each other writing about research, theory, and therapeutic practice with clients who are sexual adventurers. In an excellent and thoughtful deconstruction of the mainstream sexual culture, they explore the question of 'How did we get here?' and, further, 'How can we get somewhere better?' They propose the acceptance and honoring of the rich complexities of sexual diversity as a path for escaping the imposed shame that can constrict our lives, as they offer a wonderful guidebook to outsider sex and understanding power as an erotic resource. Read and learn from these warriors for sexual freedom as they show us how to explore our precious inner wilderness." —**Dossie Easton**, licensed marriage and family therapist; coauthor, *Radical Ecstasy: SM Journeys to Transcendence* and *The Ethical Slut*

"David Ortmann and Richard Sprott are pioneers in developing this roadmap for kink-affirmative psychotherapy. People in the BDSM community, or those practicing in secrecy, will read this book, especially the moving personal stories, and feel like they are in a support group. Professionals will have their minds—and knowledge base—opened and expanded. *Sexual Outsiders* breaks new ground." —**Margie Nichols**, PhD, executive director of Institute for Personal Growth Psychotherapy for the LGBT and Alternative Sexuality Communities

"As a sex therapist who specializes in sexual minority practices, I have read virtually every book written on BDSM in the past thirty years. *Sexual Outsiders* is truly one of a kind. The way the authors have woven in Richard Sprott's background in science with David Ortmann's clinical practice made for a very compelling read. The case studies were brilliant and kept me turning the pages in anticipation of how each story would turn out. This book is a wonderful contribution to our field." —**Neil Cannon**, PhD, certified sex therapist and couples counselor, Denver, CO

Sexual Outsiders

Understanding BDSM Sexualities and Communities

David M. Ortmann and
Richard A. Sprott

ROWMAN & LITTLEFIELD PUBLISHERS, INC.
Lanham • Boulder • New York • Toronto • Plymouth, UK

Published by Rowman & Littlefield Publishers, Inc.
A wholly owned subsidiary of The Rowman & Littlefield Publishing Group, Inc.
4501 Forbes Boulevard, Suite 200, Lanham, Maryland 20706
www.rowman.com

10 Thornbury Road, Plymouth PL6 7PP, United Kingdom

British Library Cataloguing in Publication Information Available

Library of Congress Cataloging-in-Publication Data

Ortmann, David M., 1969–
Sexual outsiders : understanding BDSM sexualities and communities / David M. Ortmann and Richard A. Sprott.
p. cm.
Includes bibliographical references and index.
ISBN 978-1-4422-1735-5 (cloth : alk. paper)—ISBN 978-1-4422-1737-9 (electronic)
1. Sadomasochism. 2. Sex (Psychology) 3. Identity (Psychology) I. Sprott, Richard A., 1965– II. Title.
HQ79.O78 2013
306.77'5—dc23
2012020483

Printed in the United States of America

"Stay gold, Ponyboy."

S. E. Hinton
The Outsiders

Contents

Foreword

Dear Mr. Ortmann,

It's taken me three weeks to write this e-mail and another week to get up the guts to send it.

I guess I need your help.

I have thoughts and ideas I don't understand. I can't say they've come out of nowhere. I guess they've always been there—kind of lurking in the background, but I was always able to keep them there and just be a normal kind of guy. I'm straight, but I guess what's happening is like what my gay buddies talk about—you know the desires are there, you know deep down who and what you are, but the shame is so great that you go about living a normal life, a Lie Life, and things seem just fine—most of the time. But you get these momentary flashes of deep desire, like nothing else—that make you feel the bottom has dropped out of your stomach. Then your heart is racing, your mouth is dry, and you feel like you did right before you had your first orgasm. The world feels scary, dark, exciting, and I feel like I'm a confused eleven-year-old all over again except more so because I'm thirty-two.

I've been normal, maybe have tried so hard to be normal, but I see things sometimes that remind me of what I really want—what really turns me on—and that stomach-dropping thing happens again. Then I know it's all as real as I am—because I'm so scared of it.

The sexual fantasies I have aren't normal, but I can't bring myself to write them down (I've been trying for those three weeks I mentioned above). I can only say that they disturb me so deeply. I can't imagine what my girlfriend, family, or friends would say if they knew. It's worse than being gay. Not that there's anything wrong with being gay. That's not what I mean. I guess what I mean is that it feels worse than any coming-out process my gay friends have ever talked about. At least they had other gay friends. I'm alone.

I feel completely outside. I feel it wherever I go and the loneliness and alienation infect my heart, my work, my body, and my relationships. It's overwhelming and if I can't talk about it soon I feel like my own shame and isolation will kill me. I think I'm sick and need to be—in some way—cured so I can live a more normal life, whatever that means.

I need to change, to be more normal, whatever that is, though I admit to you that I have little or no confidence that I can do this. I've been like this since I was just a little boy. I've never been abused—physically or sexually. I got good grades; I played baseball and ran track. I even sang in my church choir. Outwardly, my life was happy but even at that age I suffered from secrets that I couldn't share and that stayed inside of me for years. Now they won't leave me in peace. If I talk about them maybe they'll go away. If I don't talk about them, I'm afraid I will go away. I'm not afraid to die anymore.

I'm a pervert and my thoughts are bad. I was raised Catholic and even though I don't practice anymore I am convinced I am going to hell. Maybe I'm already in it. Sure feels like it.

I can't see a psychologist where I live up here in Ukiah and will travel to see you in San Francisco. That is, if you'll agree to see me. Please call me back or write me an e-mail as soon as you are able. I'm feeling a little desperate, so the sooner the better.

Sincerely yours,

Colin

Colin did come to my office and he kept coming back every week for just over three years. He was terrified of his own thoughts, feelings, and desires and even more terrified of what people would think of him if they discovered his secrets. In the course of our three years of treatment together he came to realize his desires were not so unusual nor was he in any way sick. He stopped being scared and began to develop a curiosity about himself and his sexuality that he "never had before" in his life.

Most importantly, Colin came to realize he was not alone. He was a part of a great number of men and women whose sexualities fall outside the limits of what we collectively have come to believe is normal.

These are just a few of their stories.

David Ortmann and Richard Sprott
San Francisco, CA
2012

Preface

WHAT IS BDSM ANYWAY?

It is only our third session, but working with Elaine comes naturally. Our therapeutic dialogue flows easily. She had recently terminated with another therapist, one whose name I recognized but did not know personally. She is full of questions.

"So, Harmon and I need to know, what is BDSM?" she asks.

"I am happy to answer your question, Elaine, but I find it curious that you've been tying up Harmon and doing all sorts of creative things with his bottom for years now and you don't know what BDSM is."

"Oh, I know what it *is*. I just want to know the technical definition, David."

"Well, the term *BDSM* is an acronym, actually it's a compound acronym, derived from the terms *Bondage and Discipline* (B/D), *Dominance and submission* (D/s), and *Sadism and Masochism* (S/M). It serves as a sort of umbrella label, if you will, for forms of sexuality that incorporate restraint, pressure, sensation, and elements of power exchange between the engaged parties."

"Is that really the definition?" Elaine asks.

"Well, there are a variety of definitions out there, but this is the one I like to use," I reply. "It's the most comprehensive."

Elaine was quiet and appeared to be thinking.

"So, what's it like to hear the definition of BDSM out loud?" I ask.

"Wacky. Strange. Kind of clinical," she replies. "Makes me feel like a number, or a science experiment. It doesn't sound sensual or sexy or . . ." She hesitates.

"Fun?" I venture.

"Yeah, it doesn't sound fun."

"Is it fun for you? BDSM, that is."

"Well, it has been." She deadpans. "Up 'til that definition."

Then Elaine begins to laugh, just a chuckle at first and then harder and harder—pleased with her own jest. Soon I'm giggling, too. Elaine's enjoyment of her own wit is contagious.

We're off to a good start.

Acknowledgments

David and Richard wish to thank and acknowledge the following people for helping to make this book possible:

Kevin Avila, Guy Baldwin, Frank Banks, Race Bannon, Michelle Baptiste, Michael Bettinger, boyjean, Paul Butler, Sam Caggiula, Ken Corbett, Matthew Denckla, Tiger Howard Devore, Chris Dilley, Aidan Dunn, Dossie Easton, Chris Eldredge, Kate Ellison, Ron Fouts, Chris Freed, Jeff Garner, Steven Gibson, John Gillen, David Groves, Janet Hardy, Donald Harvey, Gabrielle Hoff, Daniel Hughes, Marc Johnson, Eric Karnowski, Kathryn Knigge, Marty Klein, Keely Kolmes, David Ley, Phil Lindo, Patrick Liner, Julia Loy, Midori, Miriam Moore, Charles Moser, Patrick Mulcahey, Randy Noak, Christine Nollen, Marion Ortmann, David Ortmann Sr., Donna Molnar Pastena, David Perry, Esther Perel, Ron Pilato, David Ratner, Sean Riley, Shirley Sandler, Suzanne Staszak-Silva, David Stephenson, Gregory Sullivan, Ken Thomas, Laura Tompson, Megan Kilian Uttam, Deborah Isadora Wade, Geri Weitzman, and Ian Wolfley.

Introduction

THE BIG PICTURE

Human sexuality is a loaded topic for many people. Parents have a difficult time discussing it with their children, health education rarely covers sexually related topics (aside from the most cursory review of the reproductive system), and adults in relationships often find the subject of their own sexuality challenging to discuss and share with their partners. Although we live in a sex-saturated media culture, human sexuality is still relegated to whispered, private, and often shame-filled discussions instead of an open interactive dialogue. Even between a therapist and a patient, in the confidential confines of the therapy hour, sex is still a taboo subject, one that often elicits anxiety in both patient and therapist.

Sex is clearly a necessary biological function for the perpetuation of the species, but it is also an act of pleasure, a means of expressing passion, desire, creativity, bonding, and connection, with or without the goal of reproduction, orgasm, or even penetration. Sex requires a certain level of experience and skill in order for it to feel good.

Clumsy sex is not hot.

Sex is an ambiguous interaction; different people have varying experiences with it; people place different values, meanings, and interpretations on it. It is a beautifully complicated mess. Part of that mess is the way we put *should*s and *must*s on sex and what sex means. Sex is wrought with cultural values, a multitude of judgments and proscriptions from religious communities and governmental bodies. Moral judgments surrounding human sexuality are as old, perhaps, as human sexuality itself. Indeed, in many countries, and right here in the United States, certain forms of consensual adult sexuality are both illegal and pathologized by medical and psychological communities as mental or behavioral illnesses or disorders.

One of our tasks, both culturally and socially, is to better learn how to integrate the sexually pleasurable into our consciousness without shame or guilt. Erotic pleasure for its own sake is perfectly acceptable, and can even be a natural antidote to symptoms of anxiety or depression.

In developing a framework for addressing the concerns that arise when people explore the kinkier edges of their sexual world, it becomes important to conceptualize sex in a way that recognizes and honors its incredible complexity. We have taken steps in this book to view sexuality in the broadest and most inclusive perspective possible—a perspective that takes into account biological, cultural, psychological, philosophical, religious, and moral dimensions. This framework allows us to fully explore the variety of sexual expressions we have encountered in our work and present them for you in these pages. The development of this framework has been informed by both research and clinical experience.

THE EROTIC VERSUS THE SEXUAL: A VIEWPOINT FROM DAVID'S CLINICAL PRACTICE

The sexual and the erotic are not the same thing. In years of practicing as a psychotherapist and sex therapist, I've often let my own patients guide me in determining how they see and experience both sexuality and eroticism, how they differ and in what significant ways they complement one another.

> I often see sexuality as technicality and mechanics, whereas the erotic is more about the mystery surrounding what the mechanic might do to us.

The word *erotic* is derived from the stories of Eros, as represented in ancient Greek culture and mythology. Eros is presented in various forms within these myths. One form, the earliest form, presents Eros as the primordial creative energy in the universe. In other forms, Eros becomes a childlike god of love, causing bonds of love to form between gods and mortals. Like any child, Eros often colors outside the lines, not obeying social norms and rules.

Eroticism refers to an aesthetic focus on desire, particularly feelings of sensuality, mind-body engagement, excitement, and anticipation. The erotic is conceptual in that it thrives in a world of abstraction, imagery, and symbolism. Erotic images and ideas give form to our primordial feelings, sensations, and experiences. The erotic is subjective and playful by its very nature.

Sexuality is the embodied, more concretized way in which people experience the erotic. It inhabits the objective, biological, physiological, and physical realms. I often see sexuality as technicality and mechanics, whereas the erotic is more about the mystery surrounding what the mechanic might do to us.

We need to make the distinction between the sexual and the erotic because in BDSM, Fetish, Leather, and Kink communities[1] there are many practices and activities that are not sexual, but may be experienced as extremely erotic. Being restrained and put on display, for example, need not involve anyone's genitals or even contact between two bodies, but it can result in an intensely pleasurable and exciting experience.

OUR BINARY CULTURE

We live in a culture that emphasizes and values binary viewpoints. Something is either good or bad, healthy or unhealthy, wrong or right, light or shadow. We see this particularly with the delicate subject of sex. Someone is either male or female; an action or feeling is either normal or abnormal, right or wrong, healthy or pathological. Though these classifications appear to make things simpler, they actually serve to undermine and invalidate the wide-ranging complexities of sexual and erotic desire.

In distinguishing the sexual from the erotic, I have been forced to suspend my own preconceived notions and assumptions about sex for the purpose of seeing the erotic through the eyes of the patient or patients I am engaged with. One of the most important lessons I have learned is to recognize the pervasive existence of a cultural and sexual binary, how limiting that binary can be, and how it is shifting before our very eyes.

Within the therapy hour, through the eyes of my patients, I have seen that the landscape of sexual culture is changing, and has changed dramatically in the past decade. I also see this phenomenon outside the clinical setting, in the larger society. The public emergence of both intersex and transgender men and women, as well as the visibility of genderqueer youth who reject the traditional, binary roles of male and female, are helping us to see gender and gender identity in a more complex manner. Polyamorous[2] and other consensually nonmonogamous cultural movements have challenged us to reconceptualize how we view love, commitment, and the formation of family.

BDSM, Leather, Kink, and Fetish communities, which are also emerging more into the public eye, show us the incredible breadth of sexual expression far beyond that of traditional genital and oral intercourse. Change and evolution doesn't mean we have to lose the tradition of good old-fashioned copulation any more than we must lose the more traditional gender roles of male and female or the more classic traditions of monogamy, but we do gain an expanded sexual and erotic landscape in which to explore and play. The idea that progress forces us to leave behind what we enjoy, or believe in, is erroneous. Change can provide us with a wider array of things to choose from and enjoy.

Though sexual mechanics are important, and perhaps even more important when practicing the technical aspects of the BDSM arts, we have intentionally focused on the nature, forms, and expression of eros over the mechanics of the sexual act. We will be asking you to expand your understanding of sexuality and eroticism. We will challenge you, and ourselves, to determine how we decide whether a form of sexuality is good or bad, or if that decision is even important—or ours—to make. There have been many long-standing cultural assumptions about what can and should be seen as erotic (e.g., women with large breasts), just as there are equally strong assumptions about what should not and cannot be conceived of as erotic (e.g., being whipped or flogged). How did we come to these apparent cultural viewpoints, and how can we expand our understanding of the erotic to incorporate a wider range of individual tastes and desires?

Part of the mythology that we're questioning is the prevailing cultural assumption that forms of sexuality that fall outside social, medical, or religious norms are pathological or unhealthy, by their very nature. In a binary view of human sexuality there is "normal" and "abnormal." We are making a case for a much-less-polarized view of human sexuality, one that embraces a diversity of erotic expression.

THE SCIENCE OF SEX: A VIEWPOINT FROM RICHARD'S RESEARCH EXPERIENCE

As a scientist, I started my career by investigating the interplay between social interactions and the acquisition of language. As a topic of study, language is amazing because it is an intersection where culture, biology, the mind, and intimate social relationships all meet. When I switched from the field of child language development to the field of sexual development in adulthood, I was shocked at the difference. Child language is a very focused, organized, and well-supported area of research—there are significant graduate education programs that train the next generation of researchers and clinicians, there are clearly articulated questions and methods of investigation, and the field explores very interesting and productive theories of language acquisition. The study of sexuality, on the other hand, seems to be scattered, disorganized, and unsupported in comparison. How could something so fundamental to human nature, culture, social relationships, health, and well-being be so poorly served by science?

The area of research on BDSM, Fetish, or Kink sexuality is especially neglected. The number of scientific studies on BDSM are few, and most of them are clearly exploratory and most, if not all, are self-funded—meaning the researcher has to pay for materials and supportive services out of his or her own pocket. There are also huge gaps in the research knowledge base, mainly because of the initial stance of "sickness" and "pathology" that colors the history of how psychiatry and early sexology have explained BDSM sexuality.

The view from the scientific field is like being an explorer facing the wilderness, the unknown—we have a few maps from previous explorers, but they are not very detailed or clear, and on many of these maps there are strange spots where previous explorers have said, "Here, there be monsters."

Things have begun to change. Fields like sexology, sociology, and anthropology are further along in their investigations of BDSM sexuality and BDSM communities. Fields like psychology and psychiatry, however, are still mired in previous assumptions and older theories that clearly make a lot of assumptions of sickness or illness as a starting point. Up until recently, most of the psychological and psychiatric studies were based on a single troubled person in a specific situation. Single case studies are great for raising questions to explore, but not appropriate for providing answers. It would be similar to describing Britney Spears's Las Vegas costumes and then assuming that *all* young women dress in this fashion. Likewise, psychological and psychiatric studies of sexual predators or people suffering from Antisocial Personality Disorder are primarily the basis for studies of "sadism." These cases of people who are entangled in the criminal justice system can give a distorted view of the line between healthy and unhealthy sexuality. This forensic work, while important, can easily be misapplied to BDSM as practiced by healthy people in a vibrant subculture. For example, Hans Eysenck has charted that men convicted of sexual crimes often have very conservative, rejecting, and negative attitudes toward sexuality, seeing sex as inherently dangerous and corrupting.[3] This does not accurately describe men who are part of the BDSM subcultures in the United States, in our anecdotal experience. A proper study has yet to be done, but that lack of scientific work means that applying Eysenck's findings to a population *not* entangled in the criminal justice system is unscientific.

If all a professional sees are suffering people, it is easy to propose that all people "like that" are sick. But now we have evidence from sociology, sexology, and even some studies in psychology that clearly show that there are happy, well-adjusted people who express BDSM sexuality. I have hope that the scientific study of BDSM will continue to develop, and even flourish, in the years to come.

The view from the scientific field is like being an explorer facing the wilderness, the unknown—we have a few maps from previous explorers, but they are not very detailed or clear, and on many of these maps there are strange spots where previous explorers have said, "Here, there be monsters."

MISUNDERSTANDING AND REJECTION

Everyone's sexuality is unique. Because of that, there is always the chance that another person will misunderstand, or even reject, someone because their experience of sexuality is different. Sometimes misunderstandings themselves can lead to a sense of rejection, even when rejection is not meant or intended. Misunderstandings and rejections lead to two particular reactions: an attempt to reestablish a sense of control in the face of confusion or rejection, or an attempt to make sense of what is happening, by searching for meaning.[4]

One way to make sense of misunderstanding and rejection is to adopt the other person's attitude—to internalize the rejection, to internalize the oppression. In essence, by agreeing with the other person, one can make sense of the rejection and feel "on the same page" as the other person, and this can decrease a sense of isolation and loneliness. A person can also attempt to control their own behavior or hide the characteristic that is offending other people. Many times, people do both.

Another way to react to misunderstanding and rejection is to become angry and confront or dismiss the other person's behavior. This is part of the attempt to reestablish a sense of control. Anger also creates a larger context to understand the other person's behavior ("They're ignorant," "They're racist," etc.).

Because BDSM sexuality is often misunderstood and subsequently stigmatized and rejected, we believe the misunderstanding-rejection dynamic is a powerful factor in the lives of kinky people. The lack of knowledge and the presence of a "squick" factor on the part of partners, family members, community leaders, medical professionals, and counselors (among others) will *add* to the difficulties and stress experienced by the sexual outsider.[5]

RUNNING AWAY: THE THERAPY REFUGEE IN DAVID'S OFFICE

When a patient flees a therapeutic environment because they feel pathologized or marginalized by a clinician, we refer to them as therapy refugees. I first heard the term used by Dossie Easton, San Francisco psychotherapist and coauthor of *Radical Ecstasy*. Many of these therapy refugees have found their way to my office over the years. Traumatized and suspicious, they are in flight from a paradigm and mind-set that views them as somehow sick or maladapted because of their sexual desires, actions, or fantasies.

Whether due to fear, misunderstanding, or a lack of education, our culture has tremendous room to improve when it comes to discussing sex in a candid, open fashion, devoid of shame and judgments. The same, unfortunately, holds true for those of us in the mental health profession.

Though our professional training programs, for the most part, do an excellent job of preparing us for treating patients and helping them recover and heal, they do not do as competent a job of educating us about the breadth of human sexuality. Although *one* course in sexuality is mandatory in most counseling programs or licensing processes, the coursework is perfunctory and, due to the limited amount of time mandated for them, very basic. When we lecture on human sexuality, and BDSM sexuality specifically, in master's and doctoral-level programs, we are often struck by the lack of knowledge on the part of students and their discomfort with the topic. Gratefully, by the end, they always seem hungry for more information and more knowledge. But aside from the standard six-to-ten-hour seminar, nothing more is required of our future psychologists, therapists, and doctors.

Therapists hold a great deal of power in relationship to their clients. In the current managed-care industrial system, we have the ability to assess and to assign diagnoses that may, and often will, follow a patient throughout their lives. We have a large book, the *Diagnostic and Statistical Manual of Mental Disorders* (DSM)[6] to back us up and further strengthen that inherent power. Though the DSM has made great strides in fine-tuning the assessment and diagnostic process for therapists, we often fail to realize that it is a series of guidelines, not absolute truths. Furthermore, it is not merely a scientific or medical document. It is a manual that reflects traditional mainstream societal norms and values. It may be a medical and psychological manual, but it has also been influenced tremendously by politics, morality, and religion. Furthermore, since modern psychology and psychiatry are anything but exact sciences, the manual relies heavily on the judgments and viewpoints of the treating clinician. As clinicians, we are all too human and, try though we may, still bring our own cultural, moral, religious, and political baggage into the therapy room, which can often adversely affect our patients.

The mental health professions often begin with the assumption that kinky behavior is an expression of some mental distress. As a wise client once said to me, after a particularly negative experience with her prior therapist, "I don't have anger toward, or repressed desires for, my mom or dad, and I don't have what you guys call 'attachment issues.' I just like a good spanking. It doesn't have to mean there is something wrong with me or that there is something to be fixed. I don't want to, or need to, be fixed! Freud once said,

'Sometimes a cigar is just a cigar.'[7] Well, sometimes a spanking is just a spanking!"

Often by the time my BDSM clients find their way to my consulting room, they have already consulted with, or been in therapy with, another clinician and often with less-than-favorable results. These therapy refugees are fleeing an environment in which their sexual interests were either not understood, pathologized as a mental disorder, or made the focus of what needed to "be changed" about them to help them reach a sense of integration or peace.

These individuals come to me with a legitimate presenting problem (anxiety, depression, relationship trouble, lowered self-esteem, or communication difficulties) that now has an additional layer of trauma overlaying it from a therapy experience in which they felt, at best, misunderstood and, at worst, pathologized and marginalized. My work then becomes two-pronged: to assess the nature of the presenting problem and develop a treatment plan while assisting the client in recovering from the trauma he or she experienced at the hands of a therapist who could not be appropriately present with the diversity of his or her sexuality.

My therapy refugees come from all walks of life—straight, gay, bisexual transgender, wealthy, poor, urban, suburban, and rural—but the one thing they have in common is a deep desire to understand their sexuality, not change it, fix it, or lock it away, but to become more aware of it. My job is to create the space for that awareness to grow, a space for that inquiry to take place in a safe and contained environment, a space in which they have an ally on the journey and not a judge and jury.

LACK OF RESEARCH TO SUPPORT PATHOLOGY

Isn't wanting to be spanked, tied up, roughed up, or to experience extreme sensation a sign of some mental illness? Wanting to do those things to another person—isn't that sick? For the past 125 years, psychiatrists and psychologists have discussed sadomasochism as a mental disorder.

Until very recently, psychiatrists and psychologists discussed cases and proposed theories about the underlying psychological dynamics of SM behavior, but very little scientific work was done. Many of the statements about underlying mental illness were presented without much systematic observation and testing to support the statements, and some of these statements were adopted into the manuals that guide clinicians in diagnosing mental disorders. The fact that categories like Sexual Sadism, Sexual Masochism, and Fetishism exist in the DSM or International Classification of Diseases (ICD) doesn't mean the science behind these diagnoses is clear or present.

Lately there has been some critical review of the idea of Sexual Sadism or Sexual Masochism, as discussed in the medical literature. In fact, several Scandinavian countries have removed Sexual Sadism, Sexual Masochism, and Fetishism from their set of diagnostic categories.

The critiques include a range of positions about what should be done with these diagnostic categories. On one end, there is the position that diagnosing a sexual disorder is dangerous to people because how we think of sexual disorders is hopelessly confused and moralistic. This would mean that, given the confusion, therapists end up relying on their own personal morality rather than a body of scientific evidence. At the other end is a position that says there is some confusion, but if we live up to our ideals to practice medicine based on scientific evidence, we can refine the diagnosis of sexual disorders. Are conceptualizations of Sexual Sadism or Sexual Masochism hopelessly confused and ill-defined? Or can they be fixed? Can we use them as they are, in a way that is rigorous and ethical? We do see a small portion of people in the criminal justice system who have committed violent and nonconsensual sexual attacks on others, and the perpetrators find these attacks sexually arousing.[8] We have an intuition that something is seriously impaired, in terms of psychological functioning and character, with this kind of behavior—but exactly how is it different from a "sadist" who takes the position of a controller in a consensual scene, who causes intense sensation and pain in order to create a power exchange as part of the erotic connection?

In either case, the point is that the current situation, the current diagnostic category, can be abused and misused—either because the category itself is unclear or because therapists are ill trained to use it rigorously. This situation can lead to the labeling of people as "mentally disordered" when they are not.

Here's an example. There are statements made in the DSM that if a person has one sexual disorder like Sexual Masochism (also called a *Paraphilia*, a clinical word for a sexual disorder or dysfunction), then they are at a higher risk for exhibiting other paraphilias—which include Pedophilia. However, there are very few studies to confirm this statement—and some of these empirical, scientific studies do not support the statement. The actual evidence doesn't fit and there is no scientific consensus to back up that simple statement.[9] Yet that statement is used by courts in both criminal and civil cases, as well as other institutions in our society. That idea pervades our public understanding of sexualities and can be used in a very punitive way. But if the diagnosis of Sexual Masochism is unclear to begin with, if it conflates together healthy and unhealthy people, then we are in grave danger of harming many innocent people.[10]

TYING IT ALL TOGETHER

We would like to introduce five main messages we'll be communicating to you as we explore BDSM sexualities and communities together.

For Good or for Evil

We approach BDSM as a complex set of behaviors that can be expressions of people's health and impulses to grow, or be expressions of people's brokenness and internal conflict or suffering. One cannot tell by looking from the outside, just like one cannot tell from the outside whether a marriage is good or bad. Just because people are married, that does not tell you whether the union is healthy or unhealthy. Likewise, practicing BDSM doesn't tell you whether it's healthy or unhealthy for the person. In order to know this, you have to know what it means to the person, how it affects his or her life; you have to see the larger picture, both inside and out, before you can say anything about BDSM as a positive or negative practice.

We need to understand what the behavior is an expression of, not just what the behavior is.

At the moment we are not talking about specific actions, some of which can be damaging and unhealthy for all people. We discuss specific BDSM behaviors as healthy and unhealthy in more detail in the forthcoming chapters. For now, we are discussing BDSM sexuality as a broad general category, and in this way we cannot prejudge the sexuality as healthy or unhealthy.

Contrary to popular misconceptions that BDSM is either "good" or "bad," we believe BDSM is a neutral concept. When applied to a healthy relationship, BDSM can be playful, a growth experience, highly intimate, and gratifying. When applied to an unhealthy relationship, it can be traumatic, destructive, a barrier to intimacy, and toxic.

You Are Not Alone . . .

We believe that all healthy BDSM behavior and practice is grounded in, and surrounded by, community. There is a thriving and healthy subculture organized around BDSM in the United States and in many other countries around the world. While this is often an underground community, it has developed clear ethical values, standards, recognized practices that minimize risk, and effective ways of mentoring and educating those new to BDSM.

Practicing BDSM in isolation is dangerous, even in the age of the Internet, where people have the illusion of connection and access to information. Some of that information is good and some of the information is bad. How can you differentiate unless you have a community and culture around you that shares its wisdom and experiences?

In forthcoming chapters we detail the history, values, and organization of BDSM communities in order to help people become, and remain, connected.

. . . But You Are Unique

There is no one right way of practicing the craft of BDSM. There is no one correct way of being kinky. Many times, people feel alone when they are first coming out of the closet or exploring the edges of their sexuality. It is easy in our culture to, like Colin, feel isolated, to feel like you are the only one who gets turned on by more esoteric sexual practices. We want to assure people that they are not alone in their sexual exploration even though the ways in which they approach and practice it will vary from person to person, even within the BDSM community. We affirm the uniqueness of people's erotic landscapes by recognizing that, though many people are kinky, there is no one correct way to be so.

Though many people adopt BDSM sexuality as an intrinsic part of their identity, and construct their lives around it, there are just as many people who don't, but who are just as kinky. There is no better or worse, right or wrong, just different ways of approaching erotic self-expression. There is no one right or wrong way of building a sexual identity. It is paramount to respect people's autonomy in how they choose to build their sexual selves.

Power Is Hot

As Esther Perel asserts in her book *Mating in Captivity*, erotic desire, expectation, and excitement need space in which to grow. Differentiation, a sense of separateness and mystery, creates a dynamic in which desire can build up and then ultimately culminate in people coming together in a way that is electrifying, exciting, and orgasmic.

BDSM often uses a power differential to create that distance and mystery, the structure of which ultimately allows for an intensely connected sexual experience. BDSM is the eroticization of power. Power is a dynamic that people often try to ignore or dismiss, but its presence is undeniable in sexuality and society. Indeed, we argue that power differences have a proper place in our understanding of sexuality and society and should be welcomed and integrated. Using power, manipulating power, playing with power, identifying the presence of power is not something to be afraid of. What we ignore out of fear ultimately has more control over us than what we acknowledge, honor, and accept. Ignoring power and the impact it has on our lives doesn't make it go away.

The Dilemma of Shame

Psychology, religion, and law are just some of the social structures that can infuse sexuality with a sense of shame and secrecy. For sexualities that deviate from what is viewed as "normal" or "good," this shame can be exponential. Just as gay, lesbian, bisexual, and transgender (GLBT) communities continue to experience shame and repression in their sexual self-expression, so do BDSM communities. As sexual minorities, GLBT communities have experienced great political and social advances beyond tolerance and toward true acceptance and understanding. BDSM communities have not come that far. Those kinky closet doors remain tightly locked for many people.

The topic of shame and its impact will arise several times in this book, but here we introduce our viewpoint about shame itself. It's important to distinguish between two types of shame: healthy and toxic. Both healthy shame and toxic shame include an intense negative emotion aroused by evaluating oneself in a negative, "less than" way. Often there is the added dynamic of "being exposed" because shame develops in young children by experiencing negative evaluations from important others. The negative evaluation is intertwined with being viewed, judged, and rejected by others. The adult version would be "What would the neighbors think?!"

Healthy shame is important in the development of solidarity and connection to a family or clan, the development of moral values and behavior, and the development of a "good self"—knowing when we have crossed a line and really hurt someone else or done something that is harmful. Healthy shame is focused on embarrassment over an action, and can lead to attempts to repair and seek forgiveness or to better oneself in the future. Healthy shame involves ways to reconnect with the family or clan and thereby strengthen the group's identity and the inclusion of the person within that group.

Toxic shame causes great suffering and damages one's ability to actualize developmental potential, growth, and well-being. This kind of shame is focused on the self, the person, as somehow a failure or unlovable regardless of how one behaves or what one does. It is the difference between "I did something wrong" versus "I am wrong." The "I am wrong" toxic shame often leads people to develop compulsive tendencies and lays the ground for the development of addictions or anxiety disorders. Toxic shame dynamics can also result in people becoming overly defiant and going on the offense, as a way to defend and protect the self against the intense negative emotion. Anger and antisocial defiance can become a basic habitual stance as a result of deep, unhealthy shame.[11]

Because of ignorance, stigma, and squick reactions, people who express BDSM sexuality have to contend with risks related to unhealthy shame, and

BDSM communities have to handle the fallout from unhealthy shame. We feel that shame is often the metaphorical elephant in the room, making its presence known whether we talk about it or not.

THE ARC OF *SEXUAL OUTSIDERS*

The arc of the journey we take you on in *Sexual Outsiders* is not unlike the journey many therapists go through when working with a client presenting with a desire to better understand, or actualize, their BDSM sexuality. We begin with developing an understanding of what BDSM is, some common themes, an understanding of terminology, and a discussion of identity and roles as they play out in this sexual psychodrama. We meet the curious novice, examining some of the issues that arise when one discovers this aspect of their sexuality for the first time. We look at how common BDSM sexuality is, and delve into the communities and culture that have grown and developed around it.

We examine the process of coming out, and the role that it plays in personal, sexual, and identity development and look at some of the powerful stories from the perspectives of people going through this process. We discover some ways in which BDSM sexuality has been a healing or empowering component in an individual's life and the role of Carl Jung's concept of the Shadow and its critical role in the ownership and actualization of one's sexual fantasies.

We journey into areas where things can and do go wrong, when BDSM is counterindicated based on an individual's or relationship's toxicity or pathology. We discern the differences between BDSM and abuse. We look at the delicate strength of power exchange and its erotic role in relationships, from the most casual to the most intensive.

Finally, we unpack two of the most significant themes running throughout BDSM sexuality, that of power and that of consent. We begin an in-depth conversation about how these concepts color and mold our erotic landscape.

Most importantly, in each section, we recount the narratives of people involved in BDSM and present their voices, conflicts, accomplishments, and discoveries throughout their erotic journeys. It is their stories that bring our discussions and inquiries to life. We are most indebted to them for opening doors that have been previously closed to our understanding.

Chapter One

The Power of Language

BDSM: WHAT ARE WE TALKING ABOUT?

As I explained to Elaine, the term *BDSM* is a compound acronym derived from the terms *Bondage and Discipline* (B/D), *Dominance and submission* (D/s), and *Sadism and Masochism* (S/M). BD + Ds + SM = BDSM. It describes forms of sexuality that incorporate restraint, pressure, sensation, training, and elements of both erotic and nonerotic power exchange between the parties engaged.

What is bondage? The word conjures up images of rope and shackles, of bodies bound and struggling for release. Bondage, in its broadest sense, involves the act of restraining oneself or another using cuffs, rope, metal, fabric, shackles, or chains. An erotic feeling of immobilization or stimulation from the material and textures of the implements of restraint is one of the greatest pleasures resulting from the act of being bound. Bondage can be as simple as a pair of hands tied with a bandana or as intricate as the exquisite forms of shibari Japanese rope bondage, arts that can take years to learn and master.

Discipline is an activity in which a Dominant partner trains a submissive partner in order to produce certain behavior. Discipline incorporates rigid guidelines for behavior and involves various forms of punishment when the prescribed standards of behavior are not met.

Dominance is the state of assuming psychological or physical control over another in a power-exchange relationship, a state in which orders may be executed or services performed. The state of Dominance can last for the length of a brief, negotiated scene or for the entire length of a relationship, depending on the agreement between the Dominant and His or Her submissive. Such is the case in 24/7 "total power exchange" relationships in which people expand the power dynamic to all spheres of their relationship, all the time. Written or verbal contracts are often employed to define the length and breadth of Dominant/submissive relationships.

In contrast to Dominance, the state of submission refers to one in which an individual willingly and consensually sublimates or bequeaths his or her power to a Dominant partner in a power-exchange relationship. In doing so, the submissive allows the Dominant to take psychological or physical control over him or her. Again, this can be for several moments, an evening, or for the entire length of the relationship, depending on the agreements negotiated and agreed upon.

The myth that a submissive has no power is an erroneous, and dangerous, one. On the contrary, the state of submission may be one of the most power-ful states of BDSM consciousness for the very fact that the act of giving over one's power to a trusted Dominant partner is, in and of itself, an act of extreme power and one that should not be taken lightly. Submission should not be confused with passivity or helplessness, regardless of what it may look like. In BDSM sexuality, dynamics like submission may not be what they appear to be to the outside observer.

The terms *sadism* and *masochism* are wrought with clinical, colloquial, and historical definitions and value judgments. Named for the notorious and prolific author Donatien Alphonse François, Marquis de Sade (more com-monly referred to, simply, as the Marquis de Sade), whose sadistic imagina-tion would not fit the definition of today's consensual BDSM, *sadism* refers to the derivation of pleasure as a result of inflicting pain or watching pain inflicted on another person or persons. In the medical and psychological fields, Sexual Sadism is classified as a Paraphilia and is thus subject to scrutiny, criticism, and classification as a medical and psychological patholo-gy. The ways in which sadism, and its counterpart, masochism, have been marginalized, criminalized, and pathologized will be discussed further in the following chapters.

Perhaps lesser known than the infamous marquis, Leopold von Sacher-Masoch was the Austrian literary and philosophical figure after whom the term *masochism* was coined. A talented and extraordinarily prolific writer (he had ninety novels to his credit before his death in 1895), Sacher-Masoch is perhaps best known today for his short novel *Venus in Furs*, which detailed his own fantasies and fetishes[1] (especially for Dominant women wearing fur).[2] He was known for both writing about, and living out, his fantasies with his mistresses and wives.

In complementary contrast to sadism, *masochism* refers to the derivation of pleasure from having pain or humiliation inflicted upon oneself. Like Sexual Sadism, medical and psychological communities classify Sexual Masochism as a Paraphilia and, historically, those who subscribe to such behaviors have been pathologized, marginalized, and criminalized.

Today, the terms *Sexual Sadism* and *Sexual Masochism* are used by medical and psychological communities to describe mental illness, psychopathology, or maladaptive coping mechanisms. Within the BDSM communities, however, the terms *sadism* and *masochism* refer to consensual erotic practices from which great amounts of pleasure, sensation, and catharsis can be derived.

TERMINOLOGY: NAMES AND TITLES

The freedom and ability to name yourself, call yourself, describe—and yes, label—yourself to the world is a freedom that we hold as a crucial value to owning and feeling a sense of self, a sense of independence, or of interdependence. In naming ourselves we have the opportunity to both be a part of a culture and distinguish ourselves from it.

Throughout the course of this book you'll hear from many people. Rather than ask them to define themselves by criteria we've created, we've encouraged them to describe themselves just as they are, in that moment and in their terms. It's unlikely you'll find consistency in how the men and women who've become the voices of *Sexual Outsiders* describe themselves. We planned for, offered, invited—and embraced—this.

> So the main conflict is my birthday party, which Master wants to have at this restaurant that my training Daddy and His boy really hate. Since they don't know each other that well yet, it's hard to get them to communicate and reach some sort of compromise. It makes it even more complicated that Mistress Alexandra, who is, like, my main Mentor in the Leather community and Her girl are invited too and it will be their first meeting with everyone, including puppy seth, who is, like, my best friend. I ask you, how does a good submissive kind of . . . I don't know . . . gently take charge of a situation that is supposed to be organized by all the others . . . and, supposedly, for his pleasure. It's my birthday, after all, and all this is really frustrating!
>
> —Aaron, twenty-six-year-old leatherboy, submissive, and credit union customer services manager (Daly City, CA)

This is an actual account of a relational and communication dilemma that a patient brought up one week in therapy. Although the cast of characters may seem a mystery to anyone unfamiliar with BDSM, the basic problem is quite simple: how to get a group of people, some of whom don't know one another, to communicate and decide where to celebrate a birthday and what involvement, if any, does my patient Aaron want to have in this process? What complicates this particular scenario for someone new to BDSM culture are the array of titles and roles applied to the significant individuals in Aaron's life and a lack of understanding about how decision-making power is distributed, or not distributed, between these people. This dilemma becomes a simpler problem to comprehend with some general knowledge of BDSM terminology and specific understanding of the place these individuals occupy in Aaron's life.

So, let's unpack this. In the above account, Aaron is referring to his Master, the main Dominant male figure in his life and with whom he is in a primary relationship. Aaron also identifies a training Daddy, a man who fulfills targeted, focused, initially short-term BDSM training in ritual and protocol in order to prepare a submissive for his or her journey into BDSM. The training Daddy, in this case, also has a boy (a male identified submissive) of His own with whom He is in a primary relationship. Aaron also has a Mentor, an individual who has agreed to guide, connect, and socially sponsor a newcomer to the BDSM scene. This particular Mentor, Mistress Alexandra, also has a girl in tow (a female identified submissive) of Her own. Also in play here is a character called puppy seth, who is Aaron's best friend. Puppies are human submissives who identify as animals or pets for the purposes of submission, training, and erotic play. [3]

Rounding out this dynamic involved the revelation that Aaron's Master was ambivalent about being in charge of the birthday party and was reluctant to share the celebration with the many other people in Aaron's life, which was the crux of the conflict.

Like all subcultures, BDSM communities have co-opted vocabulary and phraseology and, in some cases, developed their own language full of terminology that can be confusing and daunting to the newcomer, be that person someone coming out into BDSM, or partners, family members, community leaders, medical professionals, or counselors seeking to educate themselves about these communities.

There is a head-spinning array of creative and colorful names for what we, the authors, have come to call the "Initiator" and the "receiver" of BDSM sex and play. Our terms correspond closely to the traditional terms *Dominant* and *submissive*, or *Top* and *bottom*, as well as to the terms from the heterosexist model of sexual intercourse: *penetrator* and *penetrated*. Now, one need not be penetrated or Dominated in the course of BDSM sexuality, or any sexuality for that matter, but these are common threads and labels running throughout this subculture's vocabulary.

A special note about the terms *BDSM*, *Kink*, and *Fetish*: to a certain extent, the use of terms like *sadism* and *masochism* and the subcultural blend of *sadomasochism* is an example of how the subculture borrowed language from the medical community to talk about itself. But these words did not arise from within the community. These terms reflect an agenda (and the stigmatizing viewpoint) of the medical and psychiatric professions. The same goes for the term *Fetish*, which was originally borrowed by psychiatrists from anthropologists. However, the words *kink* and *kinky sex* were more organic, created by early sexual minorities without relying on medical or scientific jargon.[4] So, in many ways, the term *kink* is more appropriate if one wants to honor this culture by using the terms they use to describe themselves, rather than those terms imposed on them from the outside.

Are there forms of kink and fetish sexuality that do not have a Dominant or submissive power dynamic, yet still have a partner who initiates and a partner who follows? Yes. Intense fabric bondage, such as spandex, and sensation play come to mind, where one partner is providing, or initiating, the tactile stimulation through a stimulating material and another is receiving the sensations. The play may be devoid of a D/s power dynamic, but still has an Initiator and receiver. Of course, one could make the argument that the provider of the stimulation is being Dominant and the receiver is being submissive, so the grey areas here are wide and varied. This is not science. It is culture and art, with all its richness and adaptability.

IDENTITY AND ROLES

It is important to make the distinction between what constitutes an identity and what constitutes a role. Identities are generally more fixed, whereas a role is more mutable and dependent on the specific context or activity. For example a Dominant partner may identify as a Dominant in general, not just in the course of a scene. Further to that, He or She may identify as a Sir (a female can identify as a Sir just as a male can). In the context of a scene or a BDSM psychodrama, the same Dominant may take on the role of father, coach, or prison warden, but that role tends to end when the scene ends, whereas the overarching identity of Dominant or Sir is more consistent with the individual's personality construct and process of self-identification and is, therefore, more fixed.

Similarly, a leatherboy may identify as a submissive and that identity may be one that he carries throughout his leather journey. However, in the course of a corporal punishment scene, he may find himself in the role of miscreant schoolboy or disciplined football jock, a role that he will relinquish at the end of a scene though his identity as a submissive and leatherboy remains consistently a part of his identity construct.

This is not to say identities cannot and do not change. Identities are subject to change as an individual grows and evolves in his or her path, but identities do not change with the same frequency as the many roles played within BDSM scenes.

> I get that identity is important for a lot of people in the BDSM community, but I don't get it—for myself, at least. I had a really hard time writing my Recon profile, especially after reading some of the ones that were already on the site.[5]
> It wasn't so much the activities that gave me pause. I'm comfortable with all kinds of kink and powerplay. What made me question myself was seeing all

these profiles where people were, like, "I am a slave 24/7. I never sit on furniture, eat from a dog dish, and sleep on the floor beside my Master's bed." I mean this dude was a *slave*. There were all these other profiles, Masters who said, "You will defer to Me at all times; you will be asked your opinion once and once only, and that will occur when I ask if you want to enter into a relationship with Me. I own you."

You get the picture. I'm not judging folks who live this extreme BDSM life or the fact that they adopt it as a primary part of their identity.

What bothered me was that all those profiles make me feel like a fake, a poser, some loser dabbling in BDSM. I'm an outsider among outsiders. How much does that suck? I'm not sure who I am in the kink world yet, but I am sure I'm not a Master or a slave. Those models are too rigid for me. I know I identify somewhat as a boy, but I also love Topping my Sir. Sometimes when I am fucking the sense out of Him, He calls me Sir. So what am I? I love the idea of getting caned by a Dominant woman even though I'm a gay man. What does that make me? Maybe I could play at being slave-like for the duration of a short scene, but the idea of 24/7 submission is so *not* me. I'd love to Top a sub. I'm particularly interested in flogging and impact play, but I haven't learned the skills yet. Who can I ask to teach me? Where do I go, and once I find a place or person, will they accept me as this fluid kinky dude who doesn't hold a rigid identity? Can't I just be me?

So, my therapist said to me, "No one gets to dictate what your kink looks like and you don't have to run around seeking other people's approval for who you want to be in the scene or in your life. Your identity is Samson, and Samson is always growing and evolving. That's your identity. If people ask you, and you feel like sharing, identify as an evolving kinkster—that leaves you open to everything. You can say 'yes,' or 'no,' and you're still Samson and still a valid, important part of the community. In fact, your lack of identity rigidity may be an example to others struggling with the same feelings of not fitting into a pre-fab box."

Today, I'm feeling a lot less pressure to conform. Critics who say I have to "pick a side" just get brushed aside. I've really come to believe what my therapist said. No one gets to tell me who, or how, to be. As a result, my Recon profile is a little unique but—hey—I get a lot of hits!

—Samson, twenty-six-year-old evolving kinkster, medical
student, and board game geek (Santa Fe, NM)

Like Samson, not everyone neatly identifies as exclusively Dominant or submissive. BDSM communities are noted for the many men and women who identify as versatile, or as "switches." *Switch* constitutes an identity and it is the switches who walk between the worlds, so to speak. A switch may be submissive to a Dominant partner while being the Dominant to a boy or girl of his or her choosing. The array of roles open to those who identify as switch are broad and rich.

There are, however, commonly agreed-upon terms for the many roles and identities that help define and add depth and color to the BDSM, Kink, Leather, and Fetish communities. Among the most common ones encountered are, for the Dominants: Dominant, Dom, Domme, Master, Top, Dad, Sir, Madam, Mistress, Mommy, Ma'am, Lord, and Lady. For the submissive: sub, slave, boy, girl, princess, prince, pup, son, or daughter are among some common terms. Despite specific vocabulary, there is always an Initiator and a receiver and, in most cases, a Dominant and submissive partner.

Having established this, there can be as many roles in BDSM sexuality as there are individuals to dream them up. Not surprisingly, many of these roles hearken back to classic Jungian archetypes, a topic we will explore later. In fact, BDSM culture is one of the arenas in which the modern-day inhabiting of classic mythological archetypes can be observed in full regalia.

> So, my therapist said to me, "No one gets to dictate what your kink looks like and you don't have to run around seeking other people's approval for who you want to be in the scene or in your life."

Our sexual landscape is growing and evolving, and while it does not require us to abandon the old, the tried-and-true, it does force us to reject the binary paradigm in favor of a model that allows for the breadth of sexual and erotic expression to be examined and enjoyed. We invite you to join us as we recount the ways we have come to understand and appreciate BDSM sexuality and the incredible communities that have formed around it.

Chapter Two

The Curious Novice

When Rob, a young man exploring his kink and BDSM fantasies for the first time, came to my office in late 2010, I was anticipating an average, but hopefully engaging, discussion with a BDSM newcomer. Once again, my own preconceptions of BDSM, Kink, and Fetish sexuality was broadened by this bright, curious, and engaging young man, who brought more to our discussion than I had originally anticipated.

Rob was excited about being interviewed for *Sexual Outsiders* and I am grateful to have captured, without edits, the experience of one young novice's journey.

DAVID ORTMANN: How would you describe the way you identify: gender, sexual orientation, and whether you use the term *kinky*, *fetish*, or *BDSM* or a combination of those?

ROB: It's changing. . . . FetLife.com[1] changed that a little bit, because FetLife has got this whole, like, thirty different genders, preferences, and whatnot and even though I haven't really done anything much yet, nowadays I am identifying as "hetero-flexible." Again, it hasn't come up yet, but just in terms of things I think about and fantasies, that identity is probably the case. But most of my life, and generally, I think I view the world through a pretty straight lens. One thing that I struggle with nowadays and is causing me more mental trouble, rather than BDSM, which I am pretty quickly coming to terms with, is cross-dressing, which was my first kinky behavior and interest. It was the door through which I walked through into a lot of this. That has kind of receded in importance, especially in the last few months, where I've been out in the global BDSM world and cross-dressing is falling behind in terms of importance. I mean, I am sure it's still there and I am sure it will flare up again at some point, but right now it's less important.

DAVID: I think people conflate the terms *kinky, fetish*, or *BDSM* oftentimes under one umbrella. I am just curious how it is for you, your experience of these terms and what they mean to your experience.

ROB: BDSM is one of my kinks, and is probably the most important to my identity right now. But, to me, fetishes are often things that come under that heading. I like impact play. I like cross-dressing. I like other things too and those are fetishes that fall under . . . I guess maybe, for me, kinky is the top layer, BDSM falls under that umbrella, and then my own individual fetishes follow.

DAVID: I enjoyed how you conceptualized that for me, because everybody defines these terms in relationship to his or her own experience, so there is often an interesting dialogue going on about these terms, which is helpful to me, as a therapist and in the writing of this book. So, when did you become curious?

ROB: About BDSM?

DAVID: Yes.

ROB: A long time ago. Again, it's hard for me to separate some of this out, because a lot of it bubbled up at about the same time, but cross-dressing came first and BDSM was sort of right behind it, about age thirteen, fourteen, and fifteen. I consider myself very lucky that these sort of feelings and thoughts sprouted up right around same the time my family got their first computer and Internet access. What it did for me, and which seems not to be the case for some older kinksters, is that I never really felt alone. I mean, my neighbor might not be kinky, but I knew I wasn't the only person in the world who was. I read—I've been reading a lot lately—*SM 101* by Jay Wiseman, for example. Reading his accounts thinking, "Why do I have these feelings?" And though I did have that particular question—Why do I have these feelings?—I knew I wasn't the only one out of six billion people who do. So, I have never felt that level of intense aloneness that a lot of other, older people I've talked to have experienced. I think that feeling of not being alone was valuable and good for me. I mean, there were times that I had a shitty time in high school, like everybody does, but I never felt so bad or alone that I was driven to thoughts of suicide or anything like that. At times I found it inconvenient and wished it would kind of go away, but I never felt crushed by it.

DAVID: So, are you out as being kinky, or as being someone into BDSM?

ROB: Somewhat. A lot more recently. I was out to a couple people on the Internet and then to a few dear friends, all female and one gay man. Until very recently, and this was a hang-up for me and it's less so now, I had never told a nonqueer[2] man that I was kinky, and it was hard for me to tell my gay male friend, but his coming-out process had been so difficult for him that I wanted to, somehow, reciprocate and say, "Okay, here is one of my secrets." But, up until about a year ago, I'd probably told less than half a dozen people, which was good for me after having only come out to people online. Originally, it was more coming out about cross-dressing and then about BDSM, but that balance has shifted lately. But, in the past few months, I have sort of let the ripcord go and I tell, not everybody, but I almost think more and more people knowing is inevitable because I am being more open, but I'd rather never tell my parents because at this point in my life their acceptance of this part of my life is not important to me. I mean, I don't really want to hear about their sex life. Well, if it came up . . . maybe I'd feel differently in that moment? It's not that I don't think I would be loved anymore; it would just feel weird. I don't really want to have that conversation right now. But at some point in my mind, I think it's inevitable. I told my brother, finally.

DAVID: How did that go?

ROB: It went really well. I was pleased. To back up a bit, I'd already come out to one nonqueer male already and dealt with all those possible judgments that I feared in my own head. I felt like I'd already gone over that hurdle, you know? So, in telling my brother . . . I know my brother really well, we're close, and telling him was in the wake of the final pulling of the ripcord, like I said before.

DAVID: I guess it's time to ask now: do you identify as Top, bottom, Dom, sub?

ROB: sub. I have some tiny smidge where, in a few years, I could try to Top. . . . I like the techniques of impact play so I would like to learn more about that, but I am not sure when I am going to use it. So, I got beaten and it cleared my mind wonderfully. It moved it from "This is something I fantasize about, something I may 'like'" to "This is actually happening!" You're really enjoying it and it hurts so badly, but I am not going to tell her to stop, though I know I could at any moment. I just let go and kind of floated away for a bit and I understood that what mainstream society might think about BDSM (which I think held me back from playing for a long time), now that I was experiencing it, seemed much less important.

And this, talking to you, and just being a part of the community, now seems a lot more important to me. That last beating was in January and I told my brother that night. I had to get pretty drunk to tell him (something I don't recommend for everyone . . . coming out high or drunk), but it went really well. But I am not generally out. I am out in the community. I'm out to certain friends. I was probably oversharing a little too much in the past year with people who I didn't want to share with, or who didn't understand because I was getting kind of desperate in terms of my self-expression, so I am trying to walk it back with some people, which is impossible. So, I am somewhat out, mostly with close friends and community members, and they have all been wonderful. I have not had a negative experience coming out yet, with someone I really care about, which I know is really lucky.

DAVID: How and where did you find community?

ROB: My earliest experiences were on the Internet. I had an online Mistress, which helped me with a lot of early questions and issues. But in terms of actual community, it started just this past year. I have a good friend who was having some trouble at home, so he moved in with me. It turned out, and I knew this—but never talked about it because I was scared—that he was kinky. He was much more out than I was and one day, earlier this year, we were talking about it, and I came out to him, and he was surprised, which made me glad because I felt like Super-Secret-Guy! So it rolled out from there. His very normality with the subject and his openness really helped me. I mean, here's my friend, and an artist, going to school, moving through his life, and he's so open about the kinky part of himself and it's not weird. I went to Folsom again this past year, like everyone else in the universe, and then I got beaten three times in the past year, which opens you up a bit more each time and, finally, in January, I just pulled the ripcord and said, "I want to try this!" So I had seen the website for the Society of Janus[3] for years and years and kept it in the back of my mind as something I might like to try one day.

DAVID: I just want to clarify, that when you refer to getting "beaten," are you speaking about consensual or nonconsensual contact?

ROB: Oh, completely consensual. I have a friend who has access to a lot of fun implements and was very, very nice to me. I've never been assaulted physically, against my will . . . with the exception of a few high school fights. No, this was all consensual and . . . nice. It really was. I am still buzzing off of it months later. So, back to Janus. . . . I saw they were having a membership orientation. You have to do the orientation before you can join and start taking classes. So, I went with my housemate, who I had just come out to, and his boyfriend and it was fun. The whole experience was very normalizing. So I joined and then started going to classes and more classes. I've been learning so much.

DAVID: What would you say are the top three things you're learning in these classes?

ROB: Safety, which is really important to me. I like living and want to do more of it. There are two strains of classes. One, I call my "general education BDSM classes," where there are just pages and pages of information, and then there are classes like this boot class I just took that are more hands on.

DAVID: Boot blacking?

ROB: No, boot worship. But I did take a boot blacking intensive in January. It was, like, six-hours of boot blacking! It's one of the first classes I had ever done.

DAVID: That's a lot of boot blacking for one day.

ROB: I know. I've never been really into boots, but I have found female boots attractive, especially on the right woman. The boot blacking class was more about finding new skills to add to my "service bag," but this boot worship class, even though it wasn't the pages-and-pages-of-information type of class, managed to awaken something in me that said, "I can see how people find that really hot." So, safety is number one. Number two would be learning what I like and don't like. I took three classes that were "scary" classes to me. I took a Taboo Play class, a Play Piercing class, and a Cutting class. Taboo was hot, but disturbing. Cutting squicked the hell out of me and, though I respect the power of the knife as an erotic object, I don't think I want to be cut on. And Play Piercing was a lot more fun than I thought it was going to be. I actually got pierced, just in my arm, but some of the girls there had these huge designs on their bodies that were really pretty. I didn't go in with the intention of trying it, but I wanted to, so I asked someone and they did my arms. I had just had my ears redone, and that hurt a lot, so I was afraid but play piercing is a much different sensation. It was endorphiny, and fun, and pretty. So, that was an example of liking something I didn't think I was going to like. So, I am enjoying taking a survey of the literature by taking a bunch of classes. I think that was only two, but I told a lot within those two.

DAVID: Yes, you did, and thank you. Let's look at fantasies, ones that you had when you were younger and ones you have now. Let's start with the fantasies from earlier in your life.

ROB: Kind of a lot of what I am doing now was a fantasy for a long, long time, being out and open to any extent . . . to keep what now seem like irrational fears from holding me back. It's a tough question because I am discovering such a wide selection of interests. Everything. Gosh, I mean like "Princess in the Castle," "The Knight and the Lady."

DAVID: Now, are you the Lady and the Princess or the Knight and the Prince?

ROB: At different times, I'm all of them. Though where I am at now is more of a Knight space, the serving with a purpose, being strong, and still submitting. The Princess? Well, I like pretty things, and the loss of control. The loss of control is really nice, because I am up in my own head much of the time, probably too much. And that was one of the other things about taking those beatings I told you about that was so freeing was that I was out of my head! I literally felt like I was floating physically. Hmmm . . . fantasies are hard for me to talk about because I never had that many specific fantasies. It was more of a wide range of activity interests. There are different costumes I like, and when I use costumes they tend to be female costumes, like the schoolgirl and that sort of thing. Most men's leather I don't find attractive; I don't find their boots attractive . . . but that's just me. But, yeah . . . I am not really exhibitionistic, but even that is probably changing. It might be hard for me. Actually I'll say it "will" be hard for me, in the hopes that one day it might happen. Being in public play spaces is still a little hard for me.

DAVID: What kinds of costumes do you like to play with? What costumes bring you erotic and sexual pleasure?

ROB: I feel like they're boring, in a way. Schoolgirl is always cute. A Secretary-type thing is fun.

DAVID: So these female archetypes are strong themes for you.

ROB: They are, but in actual BDSM play, costumes are less important to me, but when I do dress up, that's the way it goes right now. The flip side of that is that I like wearing suits. I like dressing up that way and I haven't invested nearly enough in suits and nice clothes like that.

DAVID: Suits are hot.

ROB: Yeah! And so it flips both ways, and part of it is that I have massive body issues. I got dragged out to Bondage-a-Go-Go[4] on Wednesday night by some scene friends that I'd told about my first planned play party that following Saturday and they were, like, "No. Come to Bondage-a-Go-Go with us on Wednesday first!" So, I got kidnapped out, which was fun. I have a scene friend who has more than a decade on me, and looks amazingly great in everything he wears. He had pants on, but he had these straps across his chest. . . .

DAVID: Like a harness?

ROB: Yes, exactly. And I was, like, "Damn! Good for you." I could never wear something like that. (a) It wouldn't look good and (b) Even if it did look good at some point in the future, and that would be nice, I'd feel so exposed! So, there's that too.

DAVID: How old are you?

ROB: I am going to be thirty soon, and I'm not nearly facing it with the trepidation I was six months before. I feel like things are aligning in my life. I feel a lot freer than I have in, well, ever.

DAVID: Well, this kind of sexuality can do that. It can be very liberating and energizing to access. Do you ever feel like you have to hide your sexuality?

ROB: Yes (pause). Yes and no. I am not in a place in my life where my parents can throw me out of the house for being who I am, and they wouldn't anyway. It might weird them out and it might be an uncomfortable conversation, but the end result would be, "We don't get it, but we love you." Which is rare.

DAVID: I think I could line up a battalion of sexual minorities who would agree with you that an experience like that is rare. That's great for you to have that kind of relationship and experience with your parents.

ROB: It is great! And it wasn't all sunshine and roses growing up but, compared with friends I've talked to, I've had a really stable, really good and loving family situation pretty much my whole life. It was a little rocky during the teenage years, which I think is true for everyone, but compared with some of the horror stories have heard from other people about their families, I am lucky. I am not religious, so I don't have some clergyperson hanging around telling me that I am going to hell. Most of the people that I am really close to know, but I am not totally out. I mean, walking down a San Francisco street in the Leather district, I am out. But walking down my suburban street, I am not out. My housemates keep wanting to fly our BDSM pride flag outside and I said, "No. We live in suburban white-bread town!" A lot of it, I know, I might be putting on myself and that may or may not fade with time. A lot of what I hide now is due to choice, about not wanting to get into conversations with people who won't understand because I don't want to have to explain it to every-one. And again, on some level . . . it's weird because I've got this internal thing, "Am I flaunting it?" Like my gay friends, I think all of them are out, even though some of them are not visibly gay, or maybe "straight-acting."

DAVID: A very popular term these days.

ROB: And some of them are definitely not "straight-acting," but if you asked all of them, "Are you out?" The answer would be wide-sweeping "Yes." I am not out on that level and I wonder, if I were, would I feel like I was flaunting it? But, just the same, I don't consider them flaunting it . . . it's just part of who they are. So, maybe I really do feel that pressure to not be completely out with everyone in my life and I don't feel com-fortable, at this point, being that out. I don't. I don't know if I ever will. I don't know that I need to wear it on my sleeve. But I know I still have a lot of societal crap to work through, those inner voices that say, "Maybe you are an outlaw" or "Maybe this is something that is weird and you should keep it tucked away in some little box." So, there's that. (pause) I don't know if I am making any sense.

DAVID: You're doing just fine. Where do you think you are going to go from here?

ROB: Well, from here, today I am going to go look at boots!

DAVID: Great.

ROB: But, in a larger sense, I had a similar question posed to me at the Society of Janus through their mentorship program and I, somewhat flip-pantly, said, "Hopefully I will have many more beatings, and many more moments of clarity so I'll know what I am doing." (pause) More play would be nice, David. I am definitely going to be taking more classes to find out what I like and enjoy. More Janus work, maybe getting involved in the organization on some level. But, that's in the future. I've thought about doing some writing, or even podcasting on the subject at some point. My ultimate goal, I guess, is really boring. I want to play house. The American Dream. I want to be married. I'd love to have kids at some point far in the future, though it can't be too far in the future 'cause time marches on. Ideally, I'd have a nice home, some job that pays the bills, maybe in the arts or in writing. Ideally, I'd be married to the Domme of my dreams. When you asked about fantasies earlier, I went through a period when I wanted to provide ultimate service, be the maid, be in a 24/7 dynamic. I mean, it sounds like it would be fun for a weekend, or even a week, or . . .

DAVID: But not necessarily a fun life?

ROB: I mean, people do it and more power to them, but I think we only pass this way once and there's a lot of stuff going on: theater, art, movies, and so many people to meet. It feels stultifying for me to be, like, "I've kept the house clean for you." And that's it? But again, whatever people do, they do. I want to have a great life, be involved in my community, meet people, talk to people, learn from them, get beaten every night—or at least as long as my body can stand it—and have a great life. My concern, one of my concerns, is that demography is against me. Being a male, a mostly straight submissive seeking a female Domme—the numbers are not very good, and this has been impressed upon me by people I've talked to, ratios I've seen at parties, in books I've read. That fills me with some trepidation, fear, and sadness, a kind of a pre-sadness. I guess part of that is trying to be a better, more interesting person . . . trying to become attractive in different ways. Remember when you asked me about the play party I went to?

DAVID: At the San Francisco Citadel?[5]

ROB: Yes.

DAVID: Your first one.

ROB: It was. Bondage-a-Go-Go was fun; it was nice to be dragged out by friends. But there was one male sub, the guy who looks great in those leather straps, and he said, "You're not the only new, shy sub here." I was able to say, "I feel less shy every day." And it's true.

DAVID: That's great.

ROB: It's *new*. It's really new, and good, and it's kind of permeating other parts of my life too, even the straight suburban middle-of-the-road part of my life. My dad and I had a disagreement over something a few months ago and I ended up saying to him, "I know who I am." And it felt true; in a way it hasn't felt true up 'til now. I do feel like I know myself and it's given me a strength and power and acceptance that is different from before I explored BDSM. It's a very new strength and power, and it's very different, a new way of looking at the world. I recommend it to everyone! I sleep better. My interactions with people have one less layer of bullshit, and I feel better! (pause) So, back to the SF Citadel and my first play party. It was fun. I didn't end up playing and I didn't really expect to. A lot of the classes I've taken, and books I've read, explain that you shouldn't really expect to play at your first play party. And that was fine. I showed up a little late in the evening. I watched a lot and talked to some new people and people I knew already. I saw a bunch of different scenes going on, mostly involving Femme Tops. Evidently there was another party the night before that was mostly male Tops, so I guess the women wanted to come out and play the next night. I saw a lot of fun stuff, like paddlings and floggings. The three scenes that really stuck with me were watching this male top that I'd seen before in classes do this really skilled whip work. It's becoming a weird kind of subfetish of mine—watching really skilled whip work because it's really intricate and beautiful to watch.

The second scene was this woman spanking a guy, and then flogging him very gently, and there was a third person kind of working with her, walking her through it, and teaching her different ways of working on her guy. It was so cute. I just stood there with this big, stupid smile on my face. It made me really happy. I am sure it would freak some people out; it would have freaked me out not long ago. But I could see, at the risk of sounding really woo-woo here, the love and the energy going back and forth between these people.

The third one that really stuck with me was this guy and this girl in a cage together for about twenty minutes. They didn't do much except kiss each other a little bit. They were both vertical, but he was up against the back of it and she was pressing up against him kind of smothering him with her body and I thought, "What a lucky bastard," because his whole world is *her* in that moment. I've been in that headspace before, though not in a scene that grand, where your world shrinks to include just the person you are playing with so intensely. In terms of the connection between those two, it was amazing to watch. To the casual passerby, it might seem so boring, like there was nothing much going on, but, if you really stopped and looked, *everything* was going on; the connection was profound. It really stuck with me, probably more than anything else I saw that night.

DAVID: It sounds like an extraordinary exchange to have witnessed.

ROB: It really was.

DAVID: So would you go back to a play party like that, at the SF Citadel or elsewhere?

ROB: Oh, yeah! I have plans to go already.

BDSM: HOW COMMON?

Often when people first become aware of unusual, non-normative, or "unacceptable" (be it explicitly stated or implicitly implied) behavior, they will ask, "Am I the only one? Are there others out there? Am I sick? Is this normal?"

Before an individual settles on any answers to these questions, they should ask themselves this significant question: "*Why* is it important to know that there are others who have had the same experiences as me?"

Certainly, most human beings want to feel less alone in their experiences, but one of the tasks of personal growth is to learn to become comfortable with one's own experiences, even if they are unusual or unique experiences. What the rest of the world is doing or experiencing, in some instances, should be less important than what the individual is experiencing. We call this an independence of experience.

Independence of experience is an aspect of autonomy. Many different theories of human development have depicted the importance of autonomy, differentiation, and even solitude. Autonomy is the ability to manage, regulate, and make choices for one's self, which may or may not be choices similar to others in their families, clans, communities, or groups. We believe autonomy is a crucial source for creativity and productivity, especially needed for people to adapt to our very complex culture. The curious novice is at a threshold of exploration that might lead to very deep and meaningful experiences of autonomy, creativity, and generativity. Like many other areas of life, one's sexuality can become a domain for such self-development.

Closely related to autonomy is the importance of authenticity. To "author" one's own life, to hold true to one's experience even in the face of disapproval or a lack of similarity to others' experience is a tremendous source of personal power. Holding true to one's experiences is a source of health and well-being and necessary to realize one's authentic self. Authenticity enables integrity and it is natural for people to want to form community, to foster a sense of shared experiences. This is where the question "Am I alone? Who else is experiencing this?" comes from. In this context, we are talking about an interdependence of experience.

The shadow-side of this interdependence of experience is the possibility of shaming, rejection, and abandonment. The interdependence of experience is a necessary part of being human but, especially for stigmatized sexualities, it can lead to higher risk for toxic shame and its consequences. The question "Am I the only one? Is this sick?" from the curious novice is an echo of the fear of rejection. Rejection and shame can drive people to either reestablish control over their lives or attempt to make sense of their experience in a new way. One risk in searching for control and meaning is to internalize the negative attitudes and rejection of others and turn against one's own experience. Several psychodynamic humanistic theories discuss very clearly how this turning against one's experience can create self-alienation and stunt personal growth, leading to significant distress and dysfunction in some cases.

The curious novice, then, is at a major developmental point in his or her life: to move toward autonomy and authenticity, or to move toward self-alienation.

The "Is this normal?" question presents yet another question a person should ask themselves: "What do we actually know about BDSM sexual interests in the general population?" In this age of increased diversity awareness and cultural competency, it is crucially important that people be educated about these forms of sexuality, outside of the often-exaggerated stereotypes. Many, if not most of us, will come across this sexual expression in our friends, family members, spouses, patients, partners, and in the media.

To find out how common or uncommon a sexual interest or behavior is, researchers have to be careful. Many people may engage in a behavior once, and never again. Does this count? On the other end, some people build entire identities around a behavior or behaviors. Many people fall somewhere in between—sometimes engaging in the behavior but certainly not identifying themselves around that behavior. So the answer to the question "Is this normal?" changes depending on how a research study decides to define what counts as *present* or *absent* based on peoples' responses.

When we ask, "How common is BDSM?" the problem is not just that people have their own interpretations and experiences that influence how they answer; it also really matters how the question is posed in the first place. If a research study asks about "biting," as Alfred Kinsey did in his groundbreaking work on human sexuality, does the researcher interpret biting as kinky or not? If a research study asks about "wrestling" versus "roughhousing" during sex, people will respond differently even though the activity is the same.

Keeping these points in mind, there have been attempts in the past to find an answer.

BDSM is an aspect that is present in approximately 23 percent of the population in terms of fantasy, at least on occasion (estimates range from 12–33 percent for women, 20–50 percent for men);[6] and expressed in behavior by 10 percent of the population at some point in their lives, and a national survey of sexual behavior in Australia found that 1.8 percent of the population had engaged in BDSM behavior within the past year.[7] A 1998 telephone survey of Australian men who had sex with men reported 12 percent of over three thousand respondents had engaged in BDSM behavior.[8] These studies have all asked about behavior without addressing questions of identity.

The relation between behavior and identity is complex and tricky, challenging research in terms of both method and theory. In terms of identity ("I'm a member of the BDSM community"), we don't have any numbers— although some community organizations in the United States like the Society of Janus or Black Rose have hundreds of members each.[9]

BDSM SUBCULTURE

One thing that is often surprising is that BDSM is not always the bizarre, isolated practice of a lone individual. There is a community that has grown around these practices, a community with a history, a language, literature, art, and a set of traditions and etiquette, all focused on BDSM behavior and BDSM identity. There is a thriving worldwide subculture.

By our estimate, there are hundreds of social and educational groups addressing aspects of BDSM in the United States, Canada, Austria, Belgium, Denmark, Finland, France, Iceland, the Netherlands, Norway, Sweden, the United Kingdom, Spain, Australia, and Germany. *Time Asia* reported on the developing BDSM subculture in China in 2001 and there is a long history of bondage as both art and play in Japan. The idea that BDSM is only a Western phenomenon is inaccurate, although there are clearly significant differences in meaning, identity, and expression when it comes to BDSM across the world.

It is very important to understand that a subculture exists around BDSM, because that subculture can provide resources and tools for sexual exploration and growth. There is a collective wisdom within the boundaries of the subculture, a wisdom that has some extremely important things to say about BDSM versus abuse, about engaging in BDSM scenes in a safe way physically, and about engaging in BDSM relationships in a safe way psychologically. Understanding the subculture allows all of us to focus on the shared values and views of the BDSM world, in order to better support and understand the sexual outsider on his or her journey.

There are several scholars who have worked to document, unearth, and examine the BDSM subculture in America. Among them are Gayle Rubin, Robert Bienvenu, and Kathy Sisson. Gayle Rubin's work has documented, in particular, the development of the gay male Leather/BDSM community in San Francisco. She has shown how a community developed in the shadows and fringes of a larger group of sexual outsiders (the gay male community).

The gay male BDSM/Leather community had its own set of practices, ethics, and understandings of BDSM behavior that did not automatically patholo- gize. Until the early 1970s, individual networks of social contacts and rela- tionships, private parties, functions, and events defined this subculture. But in the 1970s, the first "out" and organized BDSM groups, The Eulenspiegel Society (TES) and the Society of Janus (SOJ), both with political bents and educational aims, began to form respectively in New York and San Francis- co.[10]

Robert Bienvenu's work documents the development of the modern Unit- ed States BDSM and Fetish community by tracing its roots back to the early part of the twentieth century. There are two lines of development: the devel- opment of an American heterosexual Fetish/Kink cultural style that began in the late 1920s and 1930s, and a separate American homosexual Leather/ Fetish cultural development that began in the 1950s. It wasn't until the estab- lishment of social organizations with a focus on BDSM education, in the early 1970s, that these two lines of cultural development began to communi- cate, intertwine, and influence one another.[11]

Kathy Sisson has laid out the history of the modern BDSM subculture, analyzing it in terms of stages of development and the basic functions of any culture. She proposes that the present subculture is at a stage of development where it can give people a "story of origin," established codes of behavior, a way to pass down a system of shared meanings, resources, and encourage- ment for individuals to develop a sexual identity.[12]

To read these histories is to begin to gain some understanding and appre- ciation of BDSM. These histories offer us insights into the worldview and the accepted values of these communities. They remind us to view the sexual outsider in the larger context of a community. Often, the behavior of one person, when seen in isolation, comes across as a bizarre individual charac- teristic, but that behavior suddenly makes more sense when it is seen from the point of view of a community of practice, a set of traditions, rituals, and shared symbols that frame the context of the individual's actions.

SAFE, SANE, AND CONSENSUAL (SSC)

"Safe, sane, and consensual S/M" was articulated as a value in 1983 by the Gay Male S/M Activists (GMSMA).[13] It was meant to distinguish the kind of "play" that this community engaged in from any kind of harmful behavior that would make someone a candidate for a diagnosis of a mental disorder or a candidate for criminal prosecution.

Adopting the code was in direct reaction to the mainstream view that S/M was always abusive, exploitative, and coercive. This pathologizing viewpoint is exemplified by psychiatric diagnoses of Sexual Sadism and Sexual Masochism, which earlier did not make any distinction between consensual versus nonconsensual activity. The first value is named by the word *safe*. Bondage or impact play (spanking, paddling, flogging, etc.) or any other scenes or activities that create intense physical sensations would be done in a way that did not lead to injury or some ongoing physical impairment. The second value is named by the word *sane*. The roleplay or mental aspects of the scene would not cross the line between fantasy and reality. Ideally, people would not confuse the power exchange negotiated by the partners with the exercise of power outside of BDSM contexts. The third value is named by the word *consensual*. Relationships and activities within the BDSM context are negotiated before anything begins and people's stated limits are respected at all times. Partners are consulted and have opportunities to check in with one another to confirm the consent of all during the activities or relationships.

There has been an ongoing and healthy debate about the nature of safety, sanity, and consent within BDSM communities since then. Other formulations of these values have been proposed and vetted. Some in the community have objected to the word *safe* because there is always some inherent risk in any activity, and the word *safe* makes people think, especially when they are not paying attention, that there is *no* risk involved. Hence, some have proposed the term *Risk Aware Consensual Kink* or *RACK*, as a more accurate articulation of the common values of the BDSM community.

In broadening our awareness of BDSM, we must remember that there is a history and a culture behind the activities and events. The presence of communities that have articulated values like safe, sane, and consensual can be a resource for helping someone manage their involvement in BDSM activities and to distinguish healthy from unhealthy BDSM behavior.

EDUCATION AND MENTORING

One very clear value within the BDSM subculture is the importance of education and mentoring. BDSM activities involve toys, equipment, extensive roleplay, tools, and elaborate fashion. There are technical aspects to BDSM play that are unlike most other kinds of sexuality. Because of these technical aspects, there is a high value placed on skill and knowledge. This is not innate knowledge nor common sense; it is skill and knowledge that must be learned and practiced. Therefore, the need for education and mentoring is paramount if BDSM play is going to be safer and more fun.

People should understand that the BDSM community places an extremely high value on education and mentoring, and that most BDSM community organizations and social groups have a mentoring or educational component as part of the group's activities. Some of the larger groups, like San Francisco's Society of Janus or Black Rose in Washington, DC, have a clearly articulated "curriculum" or set of educational events for the curious novice. A concerned family member, friend, or partner of a curious novice should inquire as to whether or not their loved one is attending or reaching out to these community organizations or social groups.

There are also literature and websites. Several books have been written for the curious novice over the past twenty-five to thirty years. *SM 101: A Realistic Introduction*, by Jay Wiseman, and *The New Topping Book* and its companion, *The New Bottoming Book*, by Dossie Easton and Janet Hardy, are just three of several resources for the curious novice. There are hundreds of websites that are educational, not adult erotic entertainment, that present information on BDSM techniques and equipment. A list of resources is included in chapter 7.

Special note on Internet resources: There are some people who live their BDSM lives online only. There are some who read everything they can find online and then may present themselves to others as experienced and knowledgeable when it comes to BDSM technique and skill. However, most people deeply involved in the BDSM community place a very high value on in-person mentoring and education. The art and craft of BDSM is a very hands-on practice.

In 2009, the Community-Academic Consortium for Research on Alternative Sexualities (CARAS) conducted an educational needs assessment of the BDSM community (primarily within the United States).[14] Their survey had 1,405 respondents. 6.1 percent of the sample stated that they did not know anyone who could mentor them, and another 8.6 percent said that they did not get any of their BDSM education from a mentor directly—while 85.3 percent received at least some of their BDSM education from a one-on-one relationship with a mentor. By far, the majority of respondents rated mentoring as the most important source of BDSM education.

NEGOTIATION, SAFEWORDS, AND AFTERCARE

As part of the value of SSC or RACK, BDSM educational and social groups teach the curious novice about negotiation, safewords, and aftercare. Negotiation is an important set of communication and self-knowledge skills. The BDSM community stresses that people who are about to play together should discuss limits and signals to manage the safety of the scene. Limits are an expression of self-knowledge, what a person will not do, or cannot do. Each person must be able to articulate these boundaries.

Especially when someone is a novice, there may not be a lot of self-knowledge or an understanding of their own limits. Even people who have been playing for a long time might discover new limits or changed limits, after the negotiation phase and during the scene (due to physiological or health changes, for example). This is when safewords are used. During negotiation, people come to an explicit agreement of what signal means "slow down" or "stop, something is not right." A common set of signals are the words "yellow" and "red," and when said by the bottom or receiver, the Top or Initiator responds by slowing down or stopping the scene. We recognize that a big draw of BDSM is exploration—exploring the body and exploring the self. By necessity, this means dealing with the unknown, so there is always the chance of limits or boundaries being unknown at the inception, but discovered in the middle, of a scene. Safewords are a way to be safe and sane, and a way to signal consent in the middle of a scene.

"Come to the dark side; we have cookies."

Because of the possible levels of intensity reached during a play scene, BDSM educational and social groups also teach the importance of aftercare immediately following a scene or session. Physically and mentally, the bottom is not fully aware and conscious of everything that is going on within his or her body or mind. The intensity of the experience, leading to endorphins and endocannabinoids flooding the bloodstream, means that the bottom physiologically cannot be fully aware of the state of his or her body. The intensity of the experience, psychologically, means that it may take the conscious mind some time to order and process the enormity of the experience. So, a few minutes or a few hours—in some cases a few days—may pass before the bottom becomes aware of the full impact of the BDSM scene. Aftercare involves the Top or Initiator staying with the bottom and providing what is needed: water, sugar (which is why a common joke in BDSM communities is "Come to the dark side; we have cookies"), rub-downs, or soothing caresses, checking for unintentional injuries and judging awareness and orientation in terms of mental state, to know when it is safe for the bottom to function on his or her own. Aftercare also involves the Top and bottom checking in with each other within the next day or two, to communicate about their well-being after the scene.

Negotiation, safewords, aftercare, and the values of SSC or RACK are all practices and principles to manage BDSM scenes in safe and ethical ways, and these are traditions that are learned as a curious novice is socialized into the wider BDSM communities.

Chapter Three

Coming Out

IN DAVID'S OFFICE: RAY AND TROY

Ray was twenty-seven years old when he came to see me for what he described as "anxiety and some trouble with sexual confidence." He'd had anxiety for "as long as I can remember" and reported that it had been manageable until "just this year," when it began to manifest in his relationship with Troy, his boyfriend of four years. Since then, sex and intimacy had been difficult; he reported feeling as though there was a wall between himself and Troy and "I have no idea how to climb it, tear it down, or find a way around it."

Ray was remarkably calm, well-spoken, and self-reflective, exhibiting no outward observable signs of anxiety. Until recently, his sexual life with Troy was satisfying. Both men were sexually versatile and equally interested in both oral and anal intercourse. "Sex was never boring."

"Is it boring now?"

He thought for a moment, "No, not boring. Just . . . blocked."

"When did it start to feel blocked?"

"About a year ago. That's when I started feeling the wall."

"Do you feel like the wall, as you say, is being put up by Troy, by you, or some combination of the two."

"No, it's definitely me."

"So what changed a year ago?"

It was at this question that Ray began to pick at his cuticles, though he appeared consciously unaware of this. He shifted his position and sat slightly more erect. "I started surfing around on the Internet."

"And what did you find?"

"I didn't go to normal sites," he said, almost apologetically.

"What would you qualify as a normal site?"

"You know, like general oral and anal stuff. The usual gay stuff."

Ray stated that he felt nervous talking about this, but felt willing to continue. It was only our third session.

"So, Ray, you've described what these websites weren't. How about giving me a sense of what they were."

"They were sites with pictures and then stories that went along with the pictures."

"Can you tell me about the pictures and stories?"

Ray took a deep breath and jumped in. I still respect him for his courage. "They're pictures and stories of all these men tying each other up and spanking each other." He paused and exhaled. "Wow. I've never told that to anyone before."

"Even Troy?"

"Especially Troy."

"Perhaps that's contributing to the wall you feel?"

Ray nodded slightly.

"Anyhow, keep going. Tell me what these stories and images brought up for you?"

It was as though a floodgate had been opened. Ray expressed great relief after his disclosure. The images and stories he saw on the Internet aroused fantasies he'd been somewhat aware of, but had successfully repressed, for years.

"From the time I was a kid I remember how turned on I would get watching Batman and Robin, especially when they were all tied up. And in all that spandex? Comic books were my downfall! God! Any kind of spanking or discipline on television sent me spinning! I have no idea where it comes from. My mom and dad never spanked me and I have never been tied up. I never even played at cowboys and Indians as a kid."

"Perhaps the kid inside you is wanting to play cowboys and Indians now?"

I did not judge him. I let him talk. Once he disclosed his initial secret, he talked a lot. I gently interpreted and analyzed where I felt appropriate. More than anything, I listened. Just witnessing Ray's desires and letting them be in the room with us seemed to allow him some peace. But the actualization of these fantasies, the bringing to life, was still a source of frustration for him. He felt thwarted in my normalization of adult erotic powerplay because he was interpreting it solely in relation to Troy. I encouraged him to focus on himself for now, selfishly, aside from his relationship.

"Tell me what you think about when you masturbate? What is the thought or image that sends you over the edge? What makes you cum?" I get more useful information from this question than I get from any other sexual-assessment inquiry.

Ray closed his eyes. "A man is tying me up. With ropes. He's hot. He's tall and dark and dressed in black. I feel helpless and I get so hard. When he's done roping me, he picks up a big black paddle and starts whaling on my butt. By the time I get to that point, I've cum. A lot."

Validating his experience and thanking him for his honesty came easy. We discussed the images and interpreted them. We explored helplessness and what it feels like to be in power and what it feels like to have power stripped away. We talked about the history of men mentoring boys through physical and sexual hazing, from ancient Sparta through modern-day frat houses. We explored the meaning of a Dominant, controlling, disciplinary archetype in his life, and Ray disclosed his yearning for such a figure. He told me about his bottom and how incredibly sensitive it was, from his anus to his butt cheeks to the backs of his thighs.

"I want to be spanked there," he admitted. "I want to be tied up and spanked. Hard."

"Do you want to do this with Troy?"

"Yes. No . . . I am not sure. I don't know. I love him. I really do. I am in love with him, whatever that means, but I can't imagine doing that with him, let alone talking to him about it."

The focus of the work became exploring Ray's fantasies and closing the gap between him and Troy, improving their intimacy, their sex life, and connection. But the wall we kept hitting was the secret fantasies Ray was keeping from his partner.

I challenged him gently in his coming-out process and he did eventually disclose to Troy his fantasies. He invited Troy to join a couple of our sessions where Ray continued to open up more deeply and candidly.

In our three joint sessions together it became clear that Ray and Troy had a deep love and concern for one another. Their body language bespoke warmth, candor, and respect. Troy was not surprised by Ray's disclosure, feeling himself that their sex had not been satisfying for Ray for some time.

"I felt like I wasn't enough, but I didn't know what was . . . you know, enough. I guess now I do."

Troy had no interest in enacting the Dominant/submissive, Captor/captive fantasies that Ray had been harboring, but gave Ray his blessing to explore, as long as he was "safe," and that "our relationship is safe." It took them awhile to negotiate the boundaries of their relationship and what it meant for Ray to find sexual pleasure outside their heretofore monogamous model.

When he felt he was ready, I referred Ray to some local BDSM discussion and social groups, where he formed some important connections. Troy read Dossie Easton and Catherine A. Liszt's *When Someone You Love Is Kinky* and worked through some of his own personal and erotic complexities in individual therapy, as well as some of his latent judgments toward kinkier sexualities.

I cannot underline how crucial it is for someone coming out into BDSM to have loving, supportive, and curious people around them. Troy turned out to be sort of a dream partner in this instance. This scenario could have gone south had Troy not had integrity, confidence, and willingness to understand.

Ray has fulfilled his fantasies, many times over. He and Troy now have what Ray calls "great vanilla sex" and Ray has a Dominant partner, Brad, who likes to discover new ways to tie knots and spank boys.[1]

"Brad and Troy even like each other," Ray has since said to me with some amazement. "We, like, watch movies together sometimes."

Ray doesn't feel anxious anymore and expresses that what he experienced as a lack of sexual confidence was really a repression of a very creative and playful erotic desire. He calls me every couple of months to schedule what he calls "my check-in appointments . . . to see if I am still doing okay."

He is.

DYNAMICS OF COMING OUT

It can be painful and isolating, coming to the realization that there is a part of you, perhaps an important part of you, that runs right against the grain what your family, parents, partners, friends, religion, and society hold up as what it means to be a "good" person. Coming to that realization, and coping with the related stress, is a process that is unique to each person in his or her particular situation. Yet the dynamics of realizing, wrestling, claiming, owning, and perhaps even celebrating the difficult parts of you as a whole person involve similar dilemmas across people and across "rejected" behaviors. We can call this process "coming out" even when it doesn't involve bisexual or same-sex orientations. It is not much of a stretch to think of BDSM sexuality as involving a process of coming out. But what does it mean to come out as kinky, on a personal level?

> Upholding a shared worldview is central to how we cope with the realization or awareness of our own smallness, weakness, and vulnerability to death and dying.

A similar aspect that spans many different kinds of coming-out processes is the presence of a behavior or characteristic that is stigmatized by society. The conceptual work of Link and Phelan clarifies several important steps in creating a stigma, socially and psychologically.[2] For a variety of reasons, authorities and powerful, influential figures in societies begin to name or label certain behaviors or characteristics. The naming of these characteristics is a necessary first step in creating a stigma. Not everything that is given a name is stigmatized, but it is difficult for society to stigmatize anything if there is no word or label for it. For BDSM sexuality, some of the earliest words in the twentieth century connected to these behaviors and desires were *bizarre* and *kinky*. This was language created by people outside of academic and medical professions; it was the nascent field of sexology and psychiatry that invented words like *sadism, fetishism*, and *masochism* to label the behaviors and characteristics.

The next step is to connect the name or label with a negative stereotype. The label then describes part of a person, and that part comes to stand for the whole person. Taking one part of a person and using it to explain or describe who he or she is, in every action and situation, is the process of *marginalization*. We categorize the person and thereby make it easy to dismiss or reject them. If a submissive is attacked and becomes the victim of a violent crime, or domestic violence, it becomes easy for society to jump to the judgment that the submissive did something to bring it onto himself or herself, because they like to take the submissive position in erotic powerplay—the submissive must have "asked for it because they like to be the victim" or some other such dismissive conclusion. We can see a similar mind-set of blame around the sexual assault of women and girls when we think they somehow invited it by dressing in a way that can be perceived as erotic or sexy. Our categorization of the marginalized woman as a "slut," or "loose," makes it easy to dismiss the assault with, "Well when you dress like that, something's bound to happen."

But in order to create a fully realized social stigma, this dismissed or rejected person needs to be seen as part of a whole *group* that is nasty, spoiled, degenerate, evil, or sick. This is the third step, the creation of an in-group (the good people) and an out-group (the bad people). The maintenance of that boundary, that line between good and bad, enables people to clarify and claim their own identity, and to manage and maintain a "good self" which in turn helps people cope with a stressful, ambiguous, and confusing experience of reality. In some psychological theories, like terror-management theory, people raise their self-worth by showing that they are good people upholding the cultural worldview shared by the dominant social mind-set. Upholding a shared worldview is central to how we cope with the realization or awareness of our own smallness, weakness, and vulnerability to death and dying. In other words, our basic human psychology gives rise to impulses to create in-groups and out-groups, to divide people into good and bad, and to reject those bad people. It is an unconscious dynamic that is always at play in people and societies. And so the common narrative we tell ourselves is that those who get an erotic charge out of extreme sensation or intense powerplay, as a group of people, are perverted, twisted, or degenerate due to abuse or trauma early in childhood. They are a "broken" people.

The last step of stigmatization is for society to start creating rules, laws, structures, policies, and regulations that enforce a hierarchy of groups within the society. Therefore, some groups get access to resources and social capital, and other groups get less access or no access, or get lower-quality resources and less social capital. Some groups get more respect and esteem; other groups get less. Those who have higher social status are governed by "different rules" than those in lower social status groups, and often suffer different punishments or consequences when they break laws and rules. Sadism and masochism become mental illnesses categorized in the DSM or ICD; courts decide that BDSM sexuality is by definition assault on a person, and that consent has no role as a defense against the charge. In their view, no one would consent to being tied up, struck, or subjected to punishment willingly—and if they did, they must be sick and therefore unable to fully consent in the first place.

According to Link and Phelan, stigma is an expression of unequal power, and stigma is a way of preserving that situation of unequal power between different groups within a society. This way of conceptualizing stigma allows us to move from unique individual experiences, and one-to-one relating between two human beings, to the patterns and dynamics of entire societies, both levels intricately intertwined, the personal and the social.

Understanding stigma becomes central to coping with the dilemmas and stresses of personal growth when we are wrestling with parts of ourselves that have been labeled as "bad." Once we start to realize that there is a hidden aspect of us that is "spoiled" or discrediting, which opens us up to rejection, loss, misunderstanding, and even violence, we have a choice in front of us: to hide and pass, or to come out. This dilemma creates its own stress on our thinking, feeling, and relating to others. There are costs, sometimes heavy costs: do we hide and therefore maintain acceptance and access to opportunities and resources at the cost of authenticity and trust, or do we come out and therefore risk losing acceptance and access, but gain authenticity and integrity? There is no good solution to the dilemma. Hiding involves continuous vigilance, constant anxiety, and feelings of shame. Coming out involves battling society's misunderstanding, stereotyping, rejection, and aggression.

A number of psychologists have studied the process of how lesbians and gay men come out. Vivienne Cass proposed a model that rests on how a person wrestles with the incongruity between who they are in reality and the negative stereotype of the spoiled social identity. The process involves separating from the mainstream, claiming an alternative identity that is contrary to the stereotyped images of that rejected category, finding others who share that alternative sexuality, and claiming goodness and pride in that alternative. The process continues as the person integrates that former "spoiled" identity, now "good" identity, into their understanding of themselves as whole people with several roles and identities.

We argue that, for some people who feel that their BDSM sexuality is highly significant, they will need to go through a similar coming-out process.

It may be necessary to guide and support kinky people as they "separate" and challenge the stigma, and it may be necessary to guide and support kinky people as they integrate a good, healthy BDSM identity as part of who they are as whole persons. BDSM social and educational groups, kinky art and literature, networks and channels of connecting in safe environments—all of these become important for everyone to support, as they enable and encourage the process of coming out for those people who identify their BDSM sexuality as central to their way of being in the world.

Other psychological theories and approaches recognize the intricacies and the fluidity of identity formation, stating that there is no one way of coming out, and that not everyone who shares a particular characteristic (like same-sex attraction) will ultimately end up with a particular sexual identity. These newer approaches keep closer to the spirit of Erik Erikson's view of identity and its function for humans, that identity is how we create a connection to a changing society and manage that connection as we grow and evolve as individuals. Identity can never rest or stay the same, because society and individual people never stay the same from moment to moment. But connecting to others and adjusting to these fluctuations and changes is necessary for health and psychological well-being.

There is a tremendous amount of psychological theory and insight that allow us to understand the dynamics of coming out as kinky. In many ways, this process is no different than coming out as bisexual, coming out as Marxist in a Republican family, or coming out as atheist in a staunchly Catholic school. It involves resisting and reconstructing what we have been taught, reexamining what we have been told, and challenging what we have previously accepted without critical thought.

Hiding involves continuous vigilance, constant anxiety, and feelings of shame. Coming out involves battling society's misunderstanding, stereotyping, rejection, and aggression.

BDSM sexuality, like any aspect of sexuality, can be healthy or unhealthy. BDSM behaviors can be avenues for personal growth, or they can be roadblocks to well-being and connection to others. The process of coming out as a submissive or a Dominant, as a sadist or masochist or both, runs the risk of internalizing shameful, "spoiled" identities and harming one's well-being, or runs the risk of constantly battling misunderstandings and rejection from society, a dilemma that can be exhausting and wear people down. We, as individuals and professionals, can change stigma so that it is not a dilemma imposed on kinky people; we can also help our partners, friends, and family as they struggle with the stigma and dilemma put before them. We can challenge the negative stereotypes, misinformation, and ignorance around

BDSM sexuality and thereby increase the health and well-being of our entire society.

COMING OUT—A COMMUNITY ISSUE

One distinguishing aspect of BDSM sexuality and coming out, which is somewhat different from other sexualities, is that BDSM eroticizes power— and power is central to creating and enforcing stigma and oppression. As individuals grow and as a community around BDSM sexuality continues to develop, the kinky consciousness and awareness of power as an erotic re-source can translate into a critique of the negative stereotypes and stigmas created by society, at all levels. But the awareness of power and how it works also allows BDSM communities to "play" with society's stigmas. Part of the ongoing dialogue within these communities is the question about whether or not we should confront and challenge the larger society's negative view-points. Being "bad" is hot; the bad girls and the bad boys get all the fun. Engaging in forbidden and nasty behavior is hot. If you make BDSM accept-able and ordinary, integrated into society's understanding of human sexual-ity, you erase the edge, the danger, and the excitement of being outside of society. If you eroticize power, then making everyone equal or the same drains the erotic energy and destroys the point of being kinky in the first place.

A recent online interchange between members of a social media group illustrates this:

TASTER123: Part of me doesn't want vanilla society to 'get it.' I want to stay a deviant sicko (shrug).

VINCE10: I agree Taster. I'm quite comfortable being the rebel/outsider.

MARUKSA: But that sounds like you're only into BDSM because it's rebel-lious and deviant, not because it's an actual interest.

VINCE10: On the contrary, Maru. There is absolute honesty at the end of a whip. I doubt anybody gets beaten just because it's rebellious. There is, however, absolute freedom in absolutely not caring for public opinion. When one starts courting mainstream approval, it's almost inevitable that one starts editing one's behavior to meet expectations.

Of course, there are nuances and different lines and boundaries, when it comes to being healthy and kinky. Clearly, living with shame and internaliz-ing the images of an evil, disgusting personhood on an individual level is dangerous and detrimental. Not so clearly, being part of a deviant group or fringe community may not be so dangerous and detrimental, in and of itself. It does raise the risks of bad things happening, but those risks may be the price of creativity, eros, and living life in an exciting, sensational, and even meaningful way.

This is one of the underlying currents of debate within Leather, Kink, and Fetish circles. It also gets played out in the GLBT community, around whether or not same-sex marriage is a necessary part of the political agenda to rid our society of homophobic injustice. If lesbians and gay men get the right to marry, will that destroy something unique and central to what it means to be gay and lesbian in the world? This question and debate also runs through recent immigrant communities in the United States and is a thread in debates about what it means to be black in America.

Assimilation—what do we gain and what do we lose? This difficult question confronts all outsiders, including sexual outsiders.

Chapter Four

Stories of Personal Growth and Healing

DARREN AND ALICIA: THE BOY IN THE BASEMENT

I Have No Voice!

Darren, a high-level corporate executive, exuded style and confidence, even though he initially presented at my office as anxious, somewhat demanding, and (as he later confessed) "abjectly terrified." Darren was in treatment with me for three and a half months before I met his wife, Alicia. There was no intention stated, or any apparent indication for, couples therapy at our first meeting. In fact, nothing in Darren's first few sessions even related to sexuality, let alone BDSM and kink. His only comments about his marriage were, "Alicia's amazing," and "I couldn't ask for a better wife and partner." He described feeling "low self-esteem, sort of a depression, I think, and this stammering thing." The "stammering thing" referred to a speech impediment I hadn't witnessed, but was reportedly becoming a challenge to his professional career.

"It has to stop," he said. "I need your help."

He refused to tell me where he learned about my practice, saying simply, "A friend told me." After the initial assessment, a follow-up appointment, and a referral to a reputable speech therapist with whom Darren requested I work in tandem, Darren and I began to delve into his presenting problems.

He was reticent about his childhood and early life. He told me that his father had abandoned his mother and him when he was eleven years old. They formally divorced later that year. His mother raised him alone and there were no other siblings. "I did really well in school. I liked it, especially history and English." He reported his mother's death when he was age twenty with no emotion. "I lived at college anyway." Whenever I would probe for any further details about his parents, his past, or his childhood and teen relationships, he bristled and shut down. It took a lot to reengage him after these jousts, so I was very careful and intentional when I did try to explore deeper.

According to Darren, his stammer was only present when he spoke publicly and continued not to manifest in our sessions. He spoke directly and eloquently, especially regarding his career, education, and other subjects about which he felt confident, or in which he expressed pride. Darren continued to gloss over his early history, family, schooling, career, and marriage, focusing intently on what he called "the main problem": his inability to speak publicly without stammering and "getting all red in the face, which makes the stuttering worse, which just makes the whole thing horrible." Darren was convinced his depression was a result of his speaking problem.

Our sessions progressed, but I often felt stalemated by his refusal to talk about so many important and key areas of his life and social development. I wanted to understand how and where this stammer began but, when I went down that path, Darren dismissed it as a "by-product of adolescence," and one "I want to get rid of."

Darren's work with the speech therapist was moderately successful. In consultation with her, I learned that Darren developed his speech impediment around the time of his parents' divorce, when he was eleven. He reported no traumatic precedents to the initial stammer, which "took root" at "about seventh grade."

Darren, the speech therapist, and I convened for several collateral meetings that were helpful and informative, but they didn't provide the traction I thought we needed to move forward at a stronger rate than we had been, the stronger rate Darren continued to insist upon.

Still, despite continued frustration, minimal improvement, and no further personal disclosure, Darren continued to come back, week after week. Something had to be working for him.

Around the eleventh session I asked him what kept him coming back.

"I like you," he said without hesitation, but when I tried to explore the feelings behind the statement, he wouldn't join.

He did explain that, in his senior executive position with the growing Internet arm of a national brand, his public-speaking responsibilities grew over the years. When he came to me, he was delivering one speech a week in front of anywhere from twenty-five to three hundred people. "It will be three, four, and soon daily speeches, Mr. Ortmann! I need help."

Darren's urgency to "fix" the problem gave me a level of countertransferential anxiety I'd never experienced before. Yet, despite his demands that I "fix" him, I didn't feel lost or insufficient as a therapist. I just felt sad. Monumentally sad. There were moments after my appointments with Darren when I would sit in my office and weep for no apparent reason. This was not a standard reaction for me, postsession, with other patients.

I confronted him directly in our fourteenth session. "If you, as you say, want me to 'fix' you, I suggest you start opening up that steamer trunk of a life you're so committed to keeping locked up. I can only help you if you let me know you, see you."

I thought my confrontation would either calm him or cause him to walk out and never come back. I knew I was gambling.

To my relief, it calmed him. He sighed and looked down at the floor. "There are things I can't tell you yet."

There was hope implied in that *yet*.

I told him that when he was ready, I'd be here to listen.

"I don't have a voice." He led with this phrase at our very next session. He stared at the floor.

I asked him to please clarify, joining him in staring at the floor.

Gently, over the course of the session, I began to explore his statement. Though we didn't get very far with the narrative, and spent a good deal of time looking at the floor together, we made leaps in our own therapeutic alliance and in his trust of me.

As he was leaving he said, "I just don't, David. I don't have a voice." This was remarkable in that, not only did the session end on the same note as it began, but it was also the first time he had ever called me by my first name.

Enter Alicia

Darren arrived at his next appointment with a woman who he introduced as "my wife, Alicia." I smiled, welcomed her, and invited them both into my office. Internally, I was thrown. Darren hadn't warned me Alicia would be joining us and, although I have a policy that family members are welcome to visit or partake in a patient's therapy up to three sessions, I do like to know when it's happening. My instinct told me not to be rigid and start "office policy-ing" them right away. There was a reason Alicia was here, and I was sure that it would become clear. Until then, I would simply have to roll with it and process my own issues of control and feeling caught off-guard later, by myself, with fellow colleagues or in one of my consultation groups.

Alicia and Darren sat close, side-by-side in the center of my ample sofa, two sets of hands intertwined. Darren looked the most comfortable I had ever seen him. Alicia looked like she had a lot to say.

"I apologize, we apologize, for coming in together like this without warning but . . ." she began.

"I really need to be honest with you, more honest, I mean, and I am scared. Having Alicia here helps so much," Darren continued.

This was not the last time one of them would finish the sentence of the other. Unlike some of my prior experiences with couples that do this, there was no sense of them cutting one another off, or trying to dominate the conversation. It seemed natural, as though their life together was a kind of continual flowing dialogue.

"I am the friend," Alicia said simply.

"The friend?" I inquired.

"The friend who referred Darren to you."

"I am sorry I couldn't tell you," Darren said meekly, looking at me with wide eyes that reminded me of a child's. "There are a lot of things I wanted to tell you, but I couldn't find the words. Alicia can help with that. She doesn't give me words, she just makes it . . ."

"Easier for the words to be found?" she ventured.

He sighed deeply. "Yes, that's it."

"So, how did you and Darren decide on me, and where did you find me?"

They exchanged glances and nodded simultaneously. It was interesting, and new, to see a couple so conscious about, and skilled at, nonverbal communication. Alicia asked, "Do you want me to explain?"

"Yes, please. Please do." Darren exhaled in what looked like relief. There would be more of that to come.

Alicia continued, "We found your name and information on the National Coalition for Sexual Freedom's website. The Kink Aware Professionals database. We needed someone who understood our relationship and our sex life."

I nodded again, wondering how all of this was going to tie back to Darren's vocational anxiety and speech impediment, but I was quiet. I had a feeling they'd be leading me there.

"We're kinky," Darren blurted out, on the heels of Alicia's disclosure. He looked at me apologetically, as if he needed my permission to speak.

"Congratulations," I said. "How is that part of your relationship working out?"

It was as if a damn burst; they both spoke a lot, rapidly beginning and ending one another's thoughts and statements, but never with a feeling of interruption.

It was a breakthrough session in terms of the amount of information I was given, and Darren's continual sighing and smiling, which I commented on after the fourth time.

"It just feels good. No, not good. . . ."

"Freeing?" Alicia suggested.

"Yes, it feels so freeing to finally be able to talk to you like this." Darren smiled at me and then back at Alicia. This was not the Darren I had come to know over the past fourteen weeks.

Alicia and Darren, I learned, were not just kinky; they practiced BDSM as well. Playing with erotic power dynamics and exploiting power imbalances for sexual pleasure was intensely fulfilling for them. They enjoyed light bondage, blindfolds, as well as light, medium, and heavy sensation play. Sharp, cold edges and furry, feathery stroking wands were common tools of their play. They laughed and flirted as they described this aspect of their erotic world. There was no shame or reticence in their description of their colorful sex life.

They were a unique BDSM couple in many ways. There was absolutely no power differential outside the bedroom or playroom; neither identified strongly as submissive or Dominant; both said they could switch from one to the other and that "play" was truly play for them.

"When we play, we play, and we like to play hard," Alicia said. "But it *is* truly just play."

"We split the mortgage, the groceries, and process all our decisions until we come to some form of consensus," Darren continued. "It's pretty much as equitable as it can be."

"We don't only do BDSM, though," Darren said.

"Oh no, sometimes straight-up sex is great," Alicia said. "Darren can fuck me like no other man I've ever had inside me."

"Well, that sounds great for you and hopefully," I indicated Darren, "for you too."

"Oh yeah!" he exclaimed. "I can go for hours with Alicia. I love watching her cum over and over again. Sometimes when we flip, she'll put on a strap-on and fuck me till I am speaking in tongues. I never thought of myself as a multi-orgasmic man, but when Alicia nails me she hits some sweet spot inside me and I just shoot and shoot and shoot."

At this point, they were both glowing like crushed-out schoolchildren. I thought we'd developed enough of a conversational stride and sufficient trust for me to ask, "So, I have a very clear picture of everything that is working. Can you share with me what isn't working, and does any of it tie into what Darren originally came to me for: lowered self-esteem, depression, and the stammer that manifests when he has to speak publicly?"

There were only five minutes left in the session. I realize I should have timed my question better. They were thoughtful for a few moments.

Alicia began, "That's a long narrative."

"Yes," Darren said, his eyes fixed on the floor.

"David, may I come back next week with Darren?"

Darren looked right at me, with the fear and desperation I was used to seeing in his eyes, which had been absent all session. He nodded, almost pleading.

"Of course, I'll look forward to it. But let's begin by discussing how we can design this therapy to work for both of you, and for the relationship. I know my picture of it is not completely filled in yet, but before we begin that process, let's talk about how you want to continue, together, separately, or some combination of the two."

"So you're open to that?" Darren asked.

"This is your time, our time. We get to create it in the way that works best for all of us."

The Revelations

They booked a double session and arrived the following week, holding hands. In the end, every minute was needed. If I'd ever found myself wanting the full story of Darren, and Darren and Alicia, I certainly got it that afternoon.

After exchanging some pleasantries, which I had come to realize helped Darren feel at ease, they began to unfold the narrative. They both expressed that their sex life lacked for very little. The one area of dissatisfaction for them involved any impact play on Darren's bottom (spanking, slapping, paddling, or strapping). It was physically and psychologically unbearable for him.

Alicia explained, "I tried it once before I'd learned what a problem it was. It was before we were married and was very spontaneous. I gave him a big slap on his ass as he was fucking me. I mean, he's sooooo good. I was just in this primal space. I must have smacked him a good four or five times while he was fucking me. We were having really vanilla sex, but I couldn't resist spanking his bottom. He was giving me so much pleasure."

"What happened?" I asked.

"I freaked out!" Darren said. "After the third or fourth smack, I went blank, broke down, lost my erection, and cried. I went fetal. It was unexpected and humiliating."

"He was inconsolable, David," Alicia continued. "I felt truly powerless. We stopped having sex, naturally, and I just held him while he cried."

"I cried for over an hour," Darren admitted. "Having my bottom hit released something in me and once it was released there was no turning back. Alicia and I talked all night."

"What did you talk about?'"

"M-m-my m-m-mother," Darren said. It was the first time I heard the stammer and its abrupt arrival gave me chills.

We three were silent for a few seconds. It was as if a new and powerful presence was introduced to the room.

Darren and Alicia filled me in on many of the details that had been missing in Darren's account of his life. As was their pattern, they talked over and into each other, but it continued to be a comfortable patchwork conversation, except when Darren simply couldn't speak. Then he would nod to Alicia and she would continue. He continued to stammer in places and I found it endearing, compassionate, and attentive that when she was speaking, she left longer-than-natural pauses within her narrative as opportunities for Darren to reenter the conversation with enough space to accommodate his hesitancy and stammer.

Darren's father did indeed leave, but not when Darren was ten. He left when Darren was seven, and he never said goodbye. His mother showered Darren with affection, but there was no sexual abuse. She treated him, in many ways, however, like a replacement husband. They went on "dates" to the movies and were always a "couple" at family events like weddings and holiday gatherings. "I don't want you to get the idea that my mom was a pedophile, because she wasn't; she just really gave me a lot of love and attention. I liked it. It made up for the fact that that asshole left me without saying goodbye!"

The idyllic mother-son relationship changed drastically in Darren's twelfth year. "She'd say things like: I was turning out just like my father; she'd yell at me for stupid things, and then not talk to me for hours. It was a mindfuck."

Darren explained that he hit adolescence (or as he liked to say, "Adolescence hit me") early and quickly. It seemed the more his adult male characteristics emerged the more unpredictable his mother became. "One day she slapped me for spilling some iced tea on a tablecloth and sent me to my room."

Darren stopped for almost two minutes. Alicia kept her hand entwined with his. We waited.

"When she came in she made me take all my clothes off and . . ." Darren's stammer made it impossible for him to continue. He nodded at Alicia.

"It was like a Dr. Jeckel/Mr. Hyde thing, David. The moment Darren stopped being a 'boy,' his mother didn't know how to handle him, or relate to him. As if the humiliation of having to be naked in front of your mother at twelve years old weren't enough, she made him lay across the bed while she spanked him really hard with a wooden-back brush. It was the first time he'd been struck, either by her or by his father, so it came out of nowhere for him."

Naturally Darren made noise and cried and the more he did, the harder his mother hit him. She said she would teach him to be quiet. This was the first of many beatings, punishments that took on an almost ritual-like quality and increased in frequency and ferocity over time. Those first beatings also coincided with Darren beginning seventh grade, his twelfth and thirteenth year, all around the time his stammer began.

Darren was having difficulty speaking and Alicia took over. "By the time he was fourteen . . . is that right, honey?"

Darren nodded.

"By the time he was fourteen, the beatings were happening once or twice a month and with no provocation from Darren. He could never fully relax again in that house. It was as though she was angry with him for growing up and was taking all of that blind rage at Darren's father out on Darren. By then these episodes were carried out in the basement. She always beat him hard, and always on a Friday, after school, so the marks would have faded by Monday. Among other implements, she also started using an old work belt Darren's father had left behind along with some of his clothes."

I had questions as to what conditions forced Darren's father out of the house so fast, but kept them to myself for now. The cruel irony that young Darren was being beaten with the belt of the father who abandoned him was lost on none of us.

"There was no child protective services or anything. No interventions. Darren and his mom were pretty isolated, and Darren never said a word, to anyone. Until he told me everything that night after I, not knowing of course, incorporated some pretty vigorous spanking into our sex."

Darren had begun to cry. I now knew why I had spent those many moments after several of Darren's appointments weeping for no apparent reason. Yes, Darren presented as demanding, strong, and driven . . . but his sadness was almost all encompassing. Clearly during those sessions where he was fighting to stay silent, I was absorbing some of his desperate sadness.

I waited for Darren's tears to subside and tried to stay focused, but the force of the narrative made it so difficult. "Can you tell me more about the stammer. Why today? What don't I know?"

"She wouldn't let me make any noise. Ever," Darren said, stammering, and began to search for words before finally turning to Alicia.

"His mother had this crazy thing not only about beating him terribly, but also about forbidding him to cry or even make a sound. It was like that until Darren turned seventeen. He was, like, 6'2" by then and I think she was afraid of him finally, even though he'd never raised a hand to her and still felt like a frightened boy on the inside."

Darren continued, "I never made a sound. After that first beating in the bedroom with the brush and the second one in the basement, no matter how hard she hit me, I never cried. I never made a sound. I lost my voice in that basement."

The force of that statement left us all quiet for over a minute. I knew the next words must be Darren's. I believe Alicia knew it too.

"I was glad when she died," Darren said finally, not stammering. "Now I want my voice back."

"And he wants to incorporate spanking into our play sessions," Alicia said with some hesitation.

"Yeah," Darren said, "I want my voice back and my ass back! That bitch has had them for too long."

They both looked at me. I don't think I had ever felt more on the spot in my career.

"I'll bet you're wondering, 'What the hell am I going to do with these two?'" Alicia said with a good-natured smile.

"Something like that," I admitted transparently, smiling back and allowing myself to sigh slightly before I continued. "Today was a long session and I've gathered a lot of information in a very condensed period of time. I will certainly be thinking of ways to help you achieve your goals, Darren. I can't begin to thank you for your bravery today." I extended my hand and he accepted it, shaking it and holding on for another two or three seconds.

"Thank you," he said. I shook Alicia's hand and thanked her as well.

"I am going to bring you a book next week," she said by way of parting.

I heard my office door close behind them.

I sat in my chair, feeling like a wrung-out old dishrag. The session's work had been productive, groundbreaking even. The narrative, though, was extraordinarily painful and overwhelming. Countertransference is a challenge for any therapist and it was so difficult for me that day.

A part of me wanted to go back in time and give Darren's mother a right hook down a long flight of stairs. I'm not kidding. Another part of me wanted to hold and protect that young boy who now existed somehow, fully formed, in my mind. Still, not kidding. All of me wanted to somehow get Darren, boy and man, out of that basement. In my own fantasy, I guess I saw us—Darren, Alicia, and myself—as therapeutic mercenaries, soldiers embarking on something of a psychological recognizance mission.

I was grateful I had a full hour before my next patient. Darren's story still stung. It wasn't the last time I would cry following one of our sessions but, soldier or not, it was the day I wept the hardest and longest.

The Intervention

The following week Darren walked into my office like a different person. He still exuded confidence, but his presence actually felt lighter. His body held little tension and his face was relaxed. He wore a natural smile and said, "Hi, David," instead of his customary, "Hello, Mr. Ortmann."

"I think just getting all that bile out of my head helped so much. I know it was weird for me to bring Alicia here without warning that first time, but I felt like I couldn't talk. I needed her."

"I know. I am grateful she was here, and I'm grateful you're both here today."

Operating under Darren's hypothesis that his stammer and "feelings of not having a voice" were related to his maternal abuse, I knew I needed to let him lead. It was a hypothesis I was unable to agree or disagree with at this point. I'd listen and guide for now, not offer suggestions or solutions. Darren and Alicia informed me of the experiment (as they called it), an intervention they hoped would open Darren up to butt play, help him regain his voice, and allow him an outlet for the rage and betrayal he'd repressed for so many years.

Darren, not Alicia, brought out *Safe, Sane and Consensual: Contemporary Perspectives on Sadomasochism*, a book edited by Darren Langdridge and Meg Barker. It is an anthology of current thoughts on matters of BDSM, by some of the most critical thinkers in the fields of psychology and sexology. I had read several chapters, including the one they referenced as holding a potential key to their problem, Dossie Easton's "Shadowplay: S/M Journeys to Our Selves."

They had read Easton's essay several times. They asked if I had, and I told them I had.

Darren explained, "I felt something move inside me when I read the parts of 'Shadowplay' where the author described her own experiences using S/M fantasy and roleplaying as a way to heal past wounds of her own and transform traumatic events from her life into something free of shame and constraint."

Darren seemed to have no problem talking in this session, and I watched Alicia watch him with what I interpreted as pride in her eyes. She took the back seat and let him continue sharing his experience with the book.

"Those personal accounts of hers, and the one part where she talks about the woman who got out all her rage on male oppression and abuse in a safe scene with trusted male Doms, really got me thinking."

Darren was referring to Easton's account:

> We can script a scene so we get to be child, parent, brat, hero, bully, betrayer, betrayed, cops, criminals, prisoners, interrogators, priests—the possibilities are endless. We can also get to feel a particular emotion: rage, pathos, grief, shame, cunning, predatory, helpless, hapless, omnipotent. A friend of mine once set up a scene with four gay men she knew. She asked them to tie her firmly to a padded table so she could struggle as hard as she could while they flogged her and shouted every insult they could think of that men have shouted to women—cunt, bitch, on the rag, and so on. What she wanted to experience fully was her rage, and so she did, screaming and struggling, yelling back, a burning ball of fury safely tied to the safely padded table. They played it through till they were all exhausted, and my friend felt she had accomplished her purpose to completely express her rage at the sexism she had been subjected to all her life. Note that she specifically chose gay men as her tormentors—heterosexual men might have been a little too threatening. [1]

"I, we," Darren said, "want to try something like this."

I felt this was a big undertaking, and potentially full of risks, but kept those concerns to myself. I wanted to hear everything they had in mind.

Darren and Alicia explained the detailed scene they'd formulated, the execution of which, they explained, brought them to me in the first place. Darren and Alicia would conjointly remove his clothing slowly, stressing the maintenance of eye contact throughout the process. Darren would allow Alicia to restrain him to a heavily padded bench designed specifically for spanking. They showed me a photo of the piece of furniture. It was one I had seen before and knew to be safe, and sturdy, as well as comfortable for the submissive partner.

They decided on a safeword, *library*, a word unique enough vocally and syllabically to not be confused with other sounds or words that might be uttered during the course of the scene. Darren could safeword out of the scene at anytime. Further, they agreed that he would say, "It's done," when he felt the scene had had the cathartic effect they'd hoped it would.

In between the undressing and restraining and the end of the scene (or the invocation of the safeword), Darren and Alicia agreed that Alicia would spank, beat, paddle, and whip his buttocks until (a) Darren safeworded or (b) Darren said, "It's done." It was up to Alicia to use whatever force or implement she chose, though they both agreed a belt and a wooden-back brush would be used most regularly, these being the implements of Darren's childhood abuse.

The point was for Darren to experience the physical and emotional pain of his childhood in a very real and present manner. Only this time, he was encouraged to cry, scream, swear, struggle, growl, and call Alicia, his mother, or anyone, whatever name, or names, he chose. The goal was catharsis through vocalization and a reclamation of power by his consenting to the same physical and, likely, emotional pain from his youth—only this time as an adult and this time on his terms. The scene would last no more than one hour, they'd decided.

I felt many concerns, but continued to listen for now. From Darren's description of the scene, they had already committed to executing it; they were asking my help to facilitate it, answer questions, and debrief it with them in subsequent sessions. They were going to do it with or without me. They would prefer to have me "in their corner," as Darren said.

From a BDSM safety perspective I thought they had designed a safe and responsible scene and one that could easily be stopped if Darren decided. Darren's restraints could be cut in a matter of seconds in case of a fire or earthquake (I prefer to think in worst-case scenarios when assessing scene safety). A close friend knew they were doing a potentially dangerous scene and had instructions to call exactly one hour and five minutes after the scene commenced. If Alicia didn't answer, the friend was to come to their home immediately to check on her and Darren.

"Seriously," Alicia said, "I could have a heart attack or pass out. Who knows? It would be bad timing, to be sure. We have to have a wingman on call."

"Agreed," I said.

"I am completely ready and capable to provide Darren with aftercare. Is it okay to call you if one of us is upset in the hour or two following, just to have someone to talk us through the aftermath?"

"Absolutely," I agreed. "But what about your aftercare, Alicia?"

This hadn't occurred to them and I was sure, even if they achieved the results they hoped for, they both would need the hands-on care, food, tea, warmth, and objective companionship that only a very close, loving, and trusted friend could provide.

They decided to have a friend in their circle be there. Kurt already knew of their intentions with the scene. Darren called him on his cell phone from my office and Kurt agreed to serve as aftercare for Alicia and also for Darren.

Alicia and Darren decided on a day (Saturday, to allow for a full day of Sunday recovery) and a time (midafternoon) and I agreed to be on-call for two hours following the scene. They agreed to call me, even if they didn't need to, just to let me know that they were okay.

I chose this as the moment to voice some of my concerns. I felt the scene could produce the desired effect and it could also fail to. It could be a retraumatizing experience for Darren, as well as a traumatizing experience for Alicia. It could color their future BDSM play unfavorably and their relatively healthy sex lives could suffer if one, or both of them, perceived the event, or themselves, as a failure or failures. It could be psychologically liberating, or it could be frightening, harmful, and a disappointment.

"This is powerful medicine you are talking about employing." I chose my words carefully and aimed for brevity. "It could work, and it could very much *not* work. Are you ready to take this on?"

They talked through their understanding of what they were undertaking once again, with me witnessing their commitment to venture forth. By our next scheduled appointment, it would be done.

Outcome and Reflections

Alicia did call me that Saturday, fifteen minutes after their session together. Her voice was shaky and she had some difficulty finding words to describe what had happened but she was able to tell me the most important information. Both she and Darren were physically fine. Darren did not safeword and called, "It's done," a little over forty-five minutes into the scene. Darren held back from crying or yelling for about ten minutes but, as Alicia began to strike harder and more frequently, he broke down.

Alicia called Kurt seconds after Darren said, "It's done." Then she untied him, slipped freshly cleaned white briefs over him to absorb some of the blood from where his skin had broken. She wrapped him in a plush robe, put slippers on his feet, and held him tightly in her arms on the floor as she rocked him.

Kurt arrived and, having gotten a spare key from Alicia, let himself in without disrupting her aftercare.

"He hung back, just smiling and nodding once in a while. He's such a good friend."

When she'd finished rocking Darren, Kurt spent some time with both on the large sofa, arms around both of them, talking when they did and respecting the silence when they were silent.

"He took good care of us. He brought cookies, made us soup with crackers, brewed some tea, and gave us lots of water. He stayed for about two hours and took time to provide me with some much-needed aftercare. Funny, I didn't know I needed it 'til he was giving it to me. He spent some one-on-one time talking to Darren too.

"Everyone talks about aftercare and I *know* how important it is. This aftercare was unprecedented," Alicia said. "I held him and rocked him for over a half hour. I loved every second of it. I love him so much. The fact that he could share this with me, I . . ." She began to cry. I watched Darren reach over and wrap his arms around her. He planted little kisses on her forehead.

When Alicia stopped crying, she looked at Darren and they shared a gentle but lingering kiss.

"I don't even remember everything I said." Darren picked up the narrative. "The words, the cursing, the hatred, the name calling, the *hate* . . . it all just poured out of me. My mother's beatings hurt so much, but being voiceless during them hurt more."

"Oh, he yelled alright." Alicia laughed in a gentle and good-natured manner. "I heard *some language*, but I knew it was good. I knew he was getting it out. I felt safe knowing that he could safeword out at any time."

Was it arousing in any way for them, I asked.

"No, absolutely not," Alicia said. "It hurt me to hurt him that much. It was excruciating to know that his pain was very, very real, that his tears were real. They soaked the carpet beneath his head. But we made an agreement. There were many moments where I was crying, though I tried to keep that from Darren. Sometimes, I really wanted to stop, but this wasn't about me or my hurt. It was about helping him through an ordeal that, we hoped, would heal."

"No," Darren said. "Not a turn on at all. I would almost say I wasn't quite in my body, if that's possible. There was a good portion where the pain was so emotional that my rage was so high, that the physical pain was secondary. I am sure at some point my ass was numb, but my heart . . . or whatever . . .

was completely aware." He paused and continued, "It was like she'd cleaned out a very deep wound with industrial-strength alcohol. It hurt so badly at the time, but there was no doubt when it was over that the wound would, finally, heal."

Over time, it seemed to heal.

In the weeks to come, Alicia joined us less and less. Darren felt "completely comfortable" processing the work we'd completed and the work we were continuing to do on his own.

Darren's vocal impediment didn't change much in the next four to six weeks, particularly when talking about his mother. He never stammered when talking about the intervention he and Alicia shared. In three months it had diminished in frequency to warrant notice by us both. Within the year the stammer was gone from his personal life. In his professional life it continued to be an obstacle.

In troubleshooting possible interventions with Darren, I switched from my psychotherapist and sex therapist hats and pulled my old, worn social-work hat out of the mothballs. We ventured out of the office and into the field. He took me to some vacant conference rooms at his company's headquarters and I took him to some rehearsal spaces my actor and dancer friends graciously donated to me.

In these spaces we both became little boys again in the sense that we were playful and free. I refused to work on his speeches right away. Instead we did nursery rhymes and tongue twisters, we jumped up and down and sang songs of our choosing, from "Row, Row, Row Your Boat" to Led Zeppelin to Madonna—loudly and off key. This time was about *not* getting it to sound *right* or come out well. It was about finding voice. As time progressed Darren began to practice speeches in front of me and we would go over the difficult parts where he still struggled with his stammer. We explored the actual words, what they meant to him, and what psychological significance they had. We worked with his anxiety. When he would get frustrated or feel hopeless, I led him right back to singing Journey or Boston intentionally off key. We worked hard, but always accessed the playful, good humor that reminded us not to take it all, or ourselves, so very seriously.

By the next year, the corporate speeches were no longer a struggle.

As we approached the end of our work together, one day Darren said, "I feel sorry for her. It's weird but I do."

"Your mother?" I asked.

"Yeah. I mean . . . I spent so many years hating her and resenting her. I just don't anymore. I mean, what she did was fucked up, treating her son like a date, a best friend, and a substitute husband and then turning on him with a vengeance when he started to become a man, but I don't feel the rage anymore."

"What do you feel?"

"Pity. Compassion. Forgiveness, I guess. I find myself wondering what kind of a childhood she must have had and how sad and ruined a person she became."

He was silent for a bit.

"I spent so many Friday nights in that basement and so much of my adulthood was spent stuck there too."

"That's true."

"It took a lot of work and a lot of time, but I'm not trapped down in that basement anymore. Not Darren the boy, or Darren the man." He looked at me and smiled. He had tears in his eyes. "We got him out, David."

"That we did, Darren. That we did."

JUNG, CONSCIOUSNESS, AND THE SHADOW

Based almost entirely on their intuition, and with the initial help of Dossie Easton's article, Darren and Alicia found themselves exploring Darren's very deep Shadow, a disowned and unintegrated part of himself. Through the exploration, Darren was not only allowed but also encouraged to experience the full extent of his rage, confusion, fear, and sadness, the very emotions he was forced to disassociate from as a boy in order to survive his mother's abuse and his father's abandonment.

Dissociation is a basic coping mechanism that occurs when things are overwhelming. We stop ourselves from feeling or experiencing the shattering stimulation in the hopes of preserving our own integrity and sanity. The experience becomes compartmentalized, split off from the "continuous" experience of our consciousness, our *I-self*. It is like sleeping, in that there is a space or period when we are not conscious, but when we wake up on the other side of the blankness, we orient ourselves and create a "seamless" experience of ourselves and our lives. A person can see dissociation in another, or in their own personal conscious experience, when suddenly there is a lack of emotion and impulse, especially about something that would be incredibly arousing and energizing for most people. Or when there is a gap in our memory, especially about an event that would be emotionally charged. Or when suddenly it becomes difficult to concentrate and focus, but there is little emotional arousal. As a result of this mental coping action, a break or disruption in our consciousness occurs, but one that we often don't notice unless we specifically look for it. These split-off parts of ourselves find a home in what the Swiss psychiatrist and great analytic thinker Carl Gustav Jung called "The Shadow."

> No one can become conscious of The Shadow without considerable moral effort. To become conscious of it involves recognizing the dark aspects of the personality as present and real. This act is the essential condition for any kind

of self-knowledge, and it therefore, as a rule, meets with considerable resistance. Indeed, self-knowledge as a psychotherapeutic measure frequently requires much painstaking work extending over a long period.[2]

Before discussing the use of Shadow work in Alicia and Darren's case, we want to provide an overview of Carl Jung's view of the human mind. Jung describes a person's mind as having different levels. The uppermost level is Ego, the level of consciousness. This is the realm of awareness where we own, admit, and reveal those things about ourselves that are acceptable to us and safe. The next level is the Personal Unconscious. This level comprises all of the experiences, thoughts, and emotions that are too frightening, unacceptable, and overwhelming, and so they are pushed away from the Ego. This is the realm of the Shadow. The last and deepest level is the Collective Unconsciousness. This part of the mind is genetically inherited and contains basic organizing ideas that are common to all humans, across culture and across incredibly long stretches of time. Jung in particular was interested in the common organizing ideas that all human phenomenological experiences reflect, ideas that become symbolized and ritualized in similar ways across human cultures. He was also deeply interested in how the Shadow gets projected out onto other people, making social interactions illogical and driven by the unconscious emotional mind.

In Darren's case, the emotions of betrayal and rage that he experienced from his mother's abuse were so intolerable to his conscious mind that he pushed them away, as a way to survive the circumstances of his life. This overwhelming situation was also undoubtedly amplified by her forbidding him to make a sound while she beat him, thrusting him into an inescapable double-binding. To disobey her would be to invite even more punishment. To obey her would mean betraying his organic experience of the abuse, working against the hardwiring in his body and brain that when you are struck and it is painful, you yell. As is often in a case like this, a person unconsciously feels that betraying one's own experience is far safer than confronting the overwhelming destructive force bearing down. For Jung, the existence of two polar opposite motivations or ideas, as in the case of a double-bind, strongly pushes a person to dissociate.

Remember that Darren's presenting problem was difficulty in public speaking. It is difficult to speak in public, especially in an engaging way, if one cannot access the full range of one's emotions or be in touch with one's emotional self living below the level of consciousness. What comes across is robotic, or meticulously planned and rigid and ultimately artificial. Or, as with Darren, dissociation can result in difficulty finding the words, difficulty in monitoring his speech production, a "break" in the flow of his actions, due to the rising difficulty of managing his emotional arousal and his job performance all at the same time. (Please note that stammering or stuttering is not tied to anxiety alone—cases also involve organic differences in the brain unrelated to traumatic experience. There is always a combination of environmental experiences and biological differences when it comes to problems like this.)

Now, one of the most common stumbling blocks to healing from trauma and the resulting dissociation is projection. Projection is yet another defense mechanism, where the moment something touches on our Shadow parts, reminding us of what we cannot allow in ourselves, we focus outside, on the environment or other people. Suddenly we see other people as mean and cruel, but we are not mean or cruel in any way. Other people are angry, but not us! Other people are bad, spoiled, evil, outsiders. We are not. We are nothing like that; we are the polar opposite. Projections arise from inside of us but color our perception of the world. They do not arise from the real world. And since the Shadow falls on the object we are looking at, changing how it looks, we end up relating with a distorted image that is not reflective of reality. This preserves our conscious integrity—but at the cost of our growth.

The BDSM scene, and the work between Darren, Alicia, and David prior to the scene, created a space for those emotions stuck in Darren's Shadow to move into the light where they could be integrated into his personality, or his Ego. The environmental cuing of the experience through the use of BDSM techniques—but in a situation that removed the double-bind—made it acceptable to Darren to feel his full fear, confusion, and rage that had been tied to the original traumatic experience. This could not have happened if Darren had been stuck in projecting all of this anger or weakness onto others, onto the world.

The intensity of the physical impacts on the body can be understood as a way to cross the gulf of the dissociation. This might have some similarity to the dynamics underlying the phenomenon of cutting, or the nonsuicidal self-harm that has been popularly linked to adolescent girls in the past decade or so. Several studies have found that self-injury behavior is more prevalent than most people realize, with some studies finding that 12 percent to 28 percent of adolescents have experimented with cutting behavior but the behavior has been found across all ages and backgrounds.[3] Many people intentionally injure themselves, and do so at any stage of life, and injure themselves in a variety of ways. Nonsuicidal self-injury reports from people engaging in it often include references to the need both to counteract some numbness or dissociation, and to exert some control over an unbearable situation. Some studies find that an important factor is alexithymia, which is a condition wherein a person is unable to describe their feelings or put their emotional experiences into words.[4]

The clinically significant difference between nonsuicidal self-injury and the case of Darren and Alicia is that Darren and Alicia used their community ties and community-endorsed BDSM techniques in a conscious effort to grow and heal, while many people who injure themselves, as in the practice of cutting, are often doing so in isolation and not trained to do so with safety. The communal context and the intention behind the act are incredibly significant in judging the health of an action, even an action as intense as cutting or BDSM. In particular, the role of shame is crucial, as shame and embarrassment often lead those who engage in self-injury to hide their behavior or motives for the behavior. In the case of using BDSM as healing, there is notably less shame about the behavior or the motivations for the scene.

The work Darren and Alicia did together was the work of individuation, or at least part of the work of individuation. For Jung, individuation means the psychological process of integrating opposites into a larger wholeness—think of the icon for Yin and Yang as one expression of this idea. In that integration of opposites, we grow and become whole, and that wholeness allows us to be more compassionate, flexible, patient, and in touch with the deep roots of our experience of the world.

One of the main ideas we want to underscore is that BDSM is neutral. It can be used for healthy goals and motivations, or it can be expressions of suffering and dysfunction that can cause harm or prevent growth. Therefore, we can't recommend that BDSM is an appropriate tool for personal growth for everyone, or for every situation. We can't recommend that people follow Alicia and Darren's example, or the fine example of Dossie Easton in her remarkable article. But neither can we deny that some people have used BDSM for healing and growth with positive results; there are too many anecdotes to dismiss the possibility that BDSM might be useful for healing and growth for some people in some situations. Of course, there is a tremendous lack of systematic and careful research on this question, so we cannot say much more than "it seems possible."

Still, we propose that if there is going to be the possibility of healing and growth through BDSM scenes and encounters, it must be accompanied by conscious, intentional efforts to use BDSM as a tool for personal growth. It seems pretty clear that using BDSM for growth requires doing so in tandem with partners, lovers, friends, and other kinds of guidance, in order to integrate and reflect on the experience and what it means. The planning and the aftercare are crucial. If these elements are not present, then it is quite possible a person is just recreating an awful, traumatic experience with no redemption or healing.

The idea that BDSM can be used to explore the Shadow, to integrate opposites, to reclaim one's Self from brokenness and fragmentation, is an idea that is part of the folk wisdom of the BDSM communities. It may be a dangerous idea because of the potential for harm, but so are ideas like brain surgery and electricity. We entrust the actual creative use of electricity and surgery to trained experts with careful oversight and monitoring for the betterment of humanity. Perhaps with oversight and expertise, the idea of BDSM as a way to explore the Shadow and achieve healing or transformation may be a particular gift to humanity given to us by our sexual outsiders.

Chapter Five

When Things Go Wrong

DEVON AND PAT

I should have trusted my initial instincts. They don't teach that in graduate school. Trusting your instincts is not a skill you can pick up quickly; it is an art form you need to hone and craft through trial and error. I attribute my difficulties with the couple in this case scenario to my lack of experience and my newness to the world of private practice psychotherapy. I had only been in practice one year when Pat and Devon came to see me.

The presenting problem was a lack of sex and the presence of a lot of arguing. Ten minutes later they proposed a solution.

"We want to do Polyamory and BDSM. We really feel like it will enhance our sex life and we have so many fantasies we want to explore," they explained.

They had proposed the problem and the solution. They would continue to try to control our sessions from that moment forward.

By the second session the signs of one, or both of them, trying to control and manipulate the therapeutic frame became more evident. My fee was problematic. The candle in my office, though battery operated, was an allergen to one of them. The light was too bright, then too dim. I, unfortunately equally dim, found myself adjusting my environment to accommodate them. It is one of the mistakes new clinicians make, and I was making it in spades.

Devon and Pat had been in a monogamous relationship for just over one year. Pat was a recovering alcoholic with a parenting history that suggested a lack of boundaries, and Devon was a self-described survivor of sexual abuse, though was extremely vague on the details. Both were gainfully employed and reported fantasies of Kink and BDSM, which they had repressed until recently. They had begun to explore some light bondage and spanking during their recent sexual relations and were convinced that BDSM would allow them to "work out" some of the aggressions they felt in their lives and "balance out" some of the power differentials they felt. Though wanting to explore erotic power exchange, both admitted to "problems with power and inequality" due to an affiliation with the predominately liberal Bay Area politics and a commitment to social justice and equality.

My initial impressions were flooded with the heavy amount of anger in the room. Anger at me, anger at one another, anger at their parents, and anger at "the system." The system was referring to the political state of America to which they'd hitched their own ability to be happy. Constantly externalizing, I encouraged them to look more at the relationship and at themselves. In turn, they blamed me for not caring about the state of composting in America. I encouraged them to remain focused on the problems that brought them into my office to begin with and leave composting for a later time.

In short, they were beginning to piss me off.

A well-seasoned therapist, aware of his or her own countertransference, would have terminated this case, or referred the couple to a more appropriate source. Because I specialize in people who are discovering BDSM, I did not do this, thinking (and perhaps hoping) that I could help them make some headway before they left therapy (which I was convinced would be soon).

The relationship, despite being a monogamous relationship between two individuals, was already quite crowded. Pat brought Mom and Dad into almost every discussion (they'd evidently loved with little regard for boundaries) and Devon brought an entire extended family into the relationship with Pat (Devon's parents fell on the more absent/needy end of the scale than Pat's love-without-limits parentage).

More than anything the relationship felt crowded. When I tried to get the two to focus on one another, they would continue to externalize, often to hysteric proportions. The "problem" was Mom, Dad, an ex-boyfriend, me, the gardener, or George W. Bush. Highly intellectual, it was easy to get them to engage about what needed to be changed about the world, but impossible to get them to focus on what needed to be changed about them.

I became, of course, the enemy. The triangulation was inevitable and I called it out when it happened, but the ego strength to take the feedback was not there. They felt attacked and retreated. (This bonded them closer, giving some illusion of therapeutic progress.) Throughout this process, they wanted advice on how to peruse BDSM sexuality and Polyamory and I honestly shared my reluctance with them.

"I feel as though you both need to be in a more solid place with one another before incorporating others into the relationship or before introducing a powerful new kind of sexual play."

"Well, that sounds like a judgment." This is, in the Bay Area, a cardinal sin. The judgment.

"Perhaps it is. Consider it an assessment of the situation. It's what you're paying me for."

One session they offhandedly disclosed that they regularly threw objects at one another . . . ashtrays, magazines, pots . . . whatever happened to be on hand. I expressed my concern and tried to explore some more constructive ways to release anger. We were making some progress on that topic when the session came to an end. It would be our last for two weeks as I was going to a conference in New York.

Coincidentally and thankfully, I was encouraged to present a challenging case at the conference and I chose Devon and Pat. As I recounted the assessment process and our early treatment, I found myself becoming more and more angry at their villainization of me, their constant manipulation of the frame and the environment (and my allowance of that), and the fact that I couldn't, in any ethical fashion, recommend BDSM exploration or a polyamorous paradigm to this very wounded, blaming, and rageful couple. Mouths at the conference fell wide open, not at the mention of BDSM, but at my disclosure of this couple's sophisticated abuse of one another, and of me.

After some valuable feedback, I decided to give them an assessment of our work thus far and my future recommendations, which included some individual work for them both and an assertion that I didn't think introducing BDSM or Polyamory to this relationship, at this time, was wise. It was going to be a provocative session. I also decided I was through. I would refer them to another couples therapist if they wanted to continue couples work, but I had already passed my own empathetic break and did not want to address the emerging (and increasing) Axis II pathology, projections of which were beginning to make me feel uncomfortable.

In session they were incensed that I encouraged them to explore some of their own troubled dynamics before venturing into a land that involved ropes and paddles. "BDSM is powerful sexuality, and I don't think it's indicated in a relationship where there is a good deal of white-hot anger and rage."

"But we came to you because you're supposed to be the guy that tells people that BDSM is okay."

"Well then, I wish I'd known that sooner, because I am not the go-to guy for a unilateral green light on BDSM play. BDSM is neither 'okay' nor 'not okay.' It's neutral. It takes on a positive or negative cast when it is applied to a positive or negative relationship dynamic. I cannot very well encourage one of you to spank the other at night when you were throwing glasses at one another that afternoon. It would be misguided and unethical."

Again, they conceptualized the problem as me, an external object. It was unthinkable that there could be something wrong with them.

They politely and instantly terminated therapy after that session and I was happy to let them do so. I did not want to be the one to terminate. I felt it would be experienced as another wound in their already-wounded narrative. I wanted to hold the failure. I wished them the best and referred them to an appropriate referral source.

This couple was a powerful learning experience for me and helped me to honor my own boundaries regarding my fee structure, office, and environment. They helped me further solidify my belief that BDSM is a neutral entity and could be an asset or a liability, depending on the relationship. BDSM is not, and cannot be, for everyone. Nor is a polyamorous paradigm appropriate for all couples. More than anything, they taught me once and for all to trust my initial instincts.

Counterindications

Clearly, Devon and Pat were not ready to begin the journey into the pleasures and pains of BDSM. There were red flags throughout treatment that this couple might not be ready for either Polyamory or BDSM (in fact, their conflation of the two different, yet sometimes overlapping, erotic concepts was a red flag in and of itself). The deal breaker for me was the streak of white-hot anger running through the relationship like a frayed electrical cord buried under a rug, underneath an ottoman, in an empty house, during an electrical storm.

In discussing counterindications, we'd like to introduce some aspects of a clinical assessment process when evaluating either the readiness of an individual or relationship to explore BDSM, or the health of an individual or relationship already incorporating BDSM sexuality into their lives.

What is interesting and useful about these assessment questions is that they can be used by all individuals in examining the health and safety of their own relationship, partner, playmate, or even self, as well as useful in a therapeutic environment when assessing for risk, safety, or counterindications.

ABUSE VERSUS BDSM

Isn't this stuff dangerous?

Yes, it can be, but no more psychologically or physically dangerous than hiking, cycling, mountain climbing, gambling, bungee jumping, riding a motorcycle, skydiving, hang gliding, swimming in the ocean, or crossing a street. For example, in 2005 there were about 152 deaths per 1 million people in the United States from motor vehicle accidents. That same year, there were almost 2 deaths per 1 million people from accidents involving autoerotic asphyxia, probably one of the more dangerous BDSM-like activities that we can get records on. This is equivalent to the rate of people killed by a fireworks mishap, and a little less than the rate of people dying from skydiving.

In our experiences, and with years of anecdotal evidence, we can say most BDSM players are not into autoerotic asphyxia. In spite of statements made by the DSM and by some researchers who study the paraphilias, there is little evidence to support that most people who practice BDSM engage in this dangerous practice.[1] Even those who do engage often use methods that are faster in release time, like hands over mouth, rather than using things like nooses or chemical inhalants. In a survey of 350 practitioners of breath-control play, only 10 percent indicated that the practice was very important for a satisfying sexual experience, and only 10 percent engaged in the riskiest forms of auto-erotic asphyxia.[2]

All risky hobbies and activities, like BDSM, have guidelines to make participation in them safer. Involvement in adventurous activities like mountain climbing or skydiving, furthermore, are not classified as psychological disorders; involvement itself is not a symptom of any mental disease. Involvement in sexual adventures, however, can be classified as mental disorders, which underscores that the DSM is influenced by more than a psychological or scientific agenda. There are political, moral, religious, social, and legal influences, as well, in the assessment and diagnosis of mental illness.

Well, then, isn't this stuff abuse?

Sexual and physical abuses are crimes, are grave and chronic social problems, and are punishable by law in a variety of forms. What differentiates abuse from BDSM activities is the concept and practice of consent. Similar to the terms *acquiescence* and *permission*, *consent* is the process by which approval or acceptance of what is planned (often by another) is acceptable or agreeable. Consent can be granted in a number of ways, both verbal and written, formal or informal. It can also be limited by time and by context. For example, a submissive may give their consent to a Dominant partner for one evening, at a play party. Once that experience is concluded, there is no longer consent.

> The deal breaker for me was the streak of white-hot anger running through the relationship like a frayed electrical cord buried under a rug, underneath an ottoman, in an empty house, during an electrical storm.

Consent can be bestowed for longer periods of time and in the absence of a specific context. This is common with long-term relationships where consent, either articulated or implied, is a demonstration of great trust and understanding. This type of consent is most often exercised by partners who know each other very well, or have otherwise agreed to limits, boundaries, and expectations on their activities in a variety of contexts and settings.

Consent can often be formalized to the extent of developing a written contract of limits and expectations that may last for the duration of an evening or, in the case of 24/7 relationships, for the duration of the relationship (or until the period in which the next contract is composed and negotiated).

Of course, inherent in the concept of consent is the understanding and agreement upon a safeword or words for when something goes wrong. It's important to know that BDSM communities explicitly acknowledge that consent is negotiated and given at several points *during* a scene, not just at the beginning. The practice of checking on consent after a scene begins is also a characteristic that makes BDSM different from abuse.

Another aspect of BDSM scenes that distinguishes their activities from abuse is the presence of aftercare. Aftercare ratifies the consent, signaling the joint intention of the scene that just concluded. Abuse does not involve joint intention.

Having a competent knowledge of what constitutes abuse and what constitutes BDSM, and knowing how to differentiate between the two, is one of the first and most crucial aspects of the assessment process, be it a clinical assessment by a therapist or medical professional or a personal assessment by anyone involved, or becoming involved, or loving someone becoming involved, in the world and culture of BDSM.

ANGER

Anger is a powerful, activating, and often-useful emotion in both the therapeutic process and the dynamics of a healthy, growing relationship. Anger functions to motivate a person to either protect themselves when under attack or remove obstacles in their path as they move toward their goals. Anger can preserve the self and protect the journey. However, it is the way in which anger is expressed, communicated, and acted upon that can make it dangerous ground on which to explore BDSM play.

One particular concern is the intersection between anger and being in a position of power. A number of experiments and studies have found that when people are in a position of having power, their behavior and their mental state are affected in specific ways.[3] One of the clearest effects is that power leads a person to be much more likely to act, and sometimes to act impulsively. Power also tends to lessen the impact of social disapproval on one's behavior. Anger, as an emotional experience, facilitates our impulses to act and to act out. Thus, the combination of anger and being in a position of power raises the likelihood of more impulsive actions—actions that we may regret later. Given that much of BDSM is about powerplay and power negotiation, the presence of tendencies to act impulsively out of anger may be a factor that suggests that BDSM might be somewhat risky for that person.

It is also important to note that shame has a special relationship to anger. Erik Erikson noted this, as well as other psychologists like Alan Downs in his discussion of the shame and anger dynamics of gay men in his book *The Velvet Rage*. Erikson discussed anger and rebellion as a reaction to intense moments of shame, most clearly experienced as formative in a person's character during the stage of autonomy versus shame/doubt, in toddlerhood. This captures the presence of anger and shame as strong dynamics in addictions and compulsions; Erikson proposed that unstable and weak solutions to the dilemma of autonomy versus shame/doubt lead a person to develop problems with willpower. Willpower is the embodiment of the ability to choose lines of action and manage and control one's behavior. Given that much of BDSM sexuality requires significant degrees of control of one's behavior, so that doing risky and highly technical practices are done in a safer manner, problems with anger can signal problems with willpower and the control and management of one's impulses. It can signal a lack of care in enacting one's plans.

Alan Downs discusses shame, and the avoidance of shame as a felt experience, as central to understanding the psychological growth and healing of gay men. In addition, as people confront the shameful trait or characteristic in themselves, they become sensitive to the many ways in which others might misunderstand or reject them. They begin to work hard to avoid any invalidation, and to seek validation, even if the characteristic being validated by others is not really authentic to the person.[4] The dynamics can be transferable to the topic of BDSM sexuality. Pat and Devon were seeking a strong dose of validation from their therapist, and were angry they didn't get it, even if that hoped-for validation would not actually, truly affirm who they were and where they were in their relationship and personal growth.

Avoiding shame, not having fully integrated those shaming experiences into one's consciousness and self-image, can introduce a level of risk in practicing BDSM sexuality. Furthermore, since BDSM sexuality requires consciousness, healthy self-knowledge, and a high level of control if it is going to be practiced in a healthier and safer way, then the presence of impulsive anger connected to shame may be counterindicated.

ACCIDENTS

How aware do you remain in a scene?

Are you being deprived, or depriving someone else, of senses that may increase the potential for accidents or mishaps?

Are you playing on equipment? If so, has that equipment been tested for safety and sturdiness?

Are you playing in the dark? A dimly lit environment? A moderately lit environment? In an environment with exceedingly bright lights? How will these gradations of lighting affect your senses, balance, and awareness?

Are people watching, or are you playing privately? If people are watching, how close are they standing to moving toys or equipment?

What are the possible risks of falling due to lighting, equipment failure, uneven flooring, dizziness due to endorphin rushes, or paresthesia (the sensation that one's limbs are falling, or have fallen, "asleep")?

Even with the most experienced of players, accidents can happen. Just as a good driver can miss a stop sign, so can a good Dominant mis-assess a situation and potentially place their submissive partner in danger. Though the Dominant is in control of a scene, at least from most outward appearances, it is just as incumbent on the submissive to be aware of the potential for accidents, to maintain conscious awareness, to use safewords appropriately, and to communicate, both verbally and nonverbally, during a scene.

A conscious awareness and investigation of the physical environment in which BDSM scenes are enacted can help to decrease the risk for accidents. We believe that a clinician, in working with a BDSM client, should make a quick assessment about the client's level of safety consciousness—not just assessing risks for sexually transmitted infections, but assessing their level of precaution and knowledge about how to practice BDSM safely. Accident awareness is a key part of that safe BDSM practice. Accident awareness and safety are core responsibilities expected by BDSM communities.

DRUGS AND ALCOHOL

Are you partying?

And if so, what are you using, how much, and in what contexts?

Speed, meth, coke, GHB, K, poppers, marijuana, ecstasy, MDMA, alcohol, and the recreational use of prescriptions drugs are not just problems and pitfalls in BDSM communities, but also problems and pitfalls in our societies as a whole. Just as in the greater population, there are many people in BDSM communities who identify as clean and sober, and there are many who do not.

Substance use is not without its inherent dangers. However, when handling and manipulating objects such as ropes, whips, chains, gags, and duct tape, the use of drugs and alcohol becomes more dangerous, especially for the Dominant partner, who holds the physical and psychological safety of the submissive partner in His or Her hands during a BDSM scene. Like driving a car, a couple of drinks may not matter very much at all . . . until you get behind the wheel. Then it's an entirely different game, with much higher stakes. Much the same can be said for getting behind the whip or the rope in an inebriated state.

Substance use is equally dangerous territory for submissives, who may find an altered state of consciousness pleasurable but may not be aware that a high may numb their ability to gauge levels of pain and pleasure. Playing under the influence can seriously affect a sub's ability or desire to communicate with their Dominant partner should something go awry (not to mention it can affect whether they can consciously and accurately assess when something is going wrong).

Effective, connected, hot BDSM sex requires one to be in his or her right mind, grounded in his or her body, and rooted in consciousness. BDSM is inherently about connection, albeit a connection that may appear unconventional to the outside observer. Substances that cloud that connection are, at best, distractions and, at worst, dangerous.

BOUND TO PLEASE?

Are you being put into bondage? If so, what kind (rope, duct tape, irons, shackles, sleep sacks, straightjackets, cages, etc.)?

Do you have a limited range of mobility, or are you completely immobilized?

Are you additionally being deprived of any sensory awareness?

Are you gagged, or is your ability to verbally communicate limited (and to what degree), or is verbal communication impossible? If impossible, what other forms of nonverbal communication have been established beforehand to insure you can alert the Dominant of any danger you might be in?

Are you engaging in self-bondage? If so, what plans, techniques, and tools are in place (and accessible) for (a) when you wish to release yourself from bondage or (b) when you are unexpectedly forced to release yourself from bondage earlier than planned?

The erotic effects of being bound are the stuff of legend. A relatively safe activity (due in part to the lack of mobility), Dominants engaged in bondage with a submissive should retain an awareness of muscle cramping, the flow of circulation, and general comfort on the parts of Their submissives. Periodic check-ins during a scene that incorporates both bondage and flogging, for example, must cover both the intensity of the impact and the effects of the bondage on the submissive's limbs and appendages. This is standard BDSM precautionary protocol.

One of the situations in which the dangers of bondage—especially long-term bondage and bondage that utilizes sleep sacks, straightjackets, or other forms of multiple sensory deprivations—become magnified is when the submissive is left alone. Although this form of long-term restraint play is erotic for many, for the sake of safety, it is important that the Dominant not stray too far and check in regularly with their bound sub.

So perhaps one of the most important questions is: are you being left alone?

If so, can you free yourself without the assistance of the Dominant?

Are doors (particularly in private environments, like playrooms, bedrooms, and home dungeons) locked or unlocked?

In short, were there a fire, or an earthquake, a tornado, or other unplanned emergency, how quickly could your mobility and senses be restored to fully functioning order?

With regard to bondage and being left or leaving someone alone, a worst-case scenario contingency plan is best maintained.

LESSONS LEARNED

If you are a kinky person, or love someone who is kinky, and are concerned about whether or not he or she should be engaging in this kind of play, then we hope the above set of questions and ideas give you a starting point in your discussions and discernments. Lack of consent and the mismanagement of consent, lack of technical skills and safety practices when doing complex scenes or using toys/tools with a potential for dangerous consequences, unexamined or unconscious anger and shame, the presence of drugs/alcohol in play, and being left alone or practicing play alone—these are the most obvious signs that BDSM presents a higher risk than it should.

All of these possible indicators of higher risk can be addressed and even alleviated by active involvement in the BDSM community. We again come back to one of our main messages, "You are not alone." Healthy BDSM behavior is much more likely when a person is connected and integrated into the organized BDSM community. It is here that a person can learn how to manage consent, learn technical skills, and figure out how to address the internalized shame and anger that arises from having to deal with stigma and the threat of rejection. It is in community that we can avoid the dangers of playing alone, or making sure that alcohol or drugs are not impairing our judgment in a scene (many organized play spaces and dungeons, and events or parties, have dungeon monitors who enforce rules against playing while impaired).

> If you make the rollercoaster too safe, it might as well be a merry-go-round.

While we believe the above issues are good starting points in deciding whether or not BDSM sexuality may be a healthy choice (for a particular person, in a particular moment in time, in a particular place), we also want to acknowledge that the topic of risk, and whether or not someone should be doing some particular BDSM activity, is a very sensitive and difficult one for BDSM communities. There have been many discussions and arguments around "safe, sane, and consensual" (SSC) as inadequately capturing the ethics and values of the community's BDSM practices, with some communities' members arguing that erotic powerplay and intense sensation scenes always carry a level of risk. They argue for the replacement of SSC with RACK: Risk-Aware Consensual Kink. Others argue that "safe" is an impossible goal and drains the erotic thrill found in playing with risk or danger—if you make the rollercoaster too safe, it might as well be a merry-go-round. If a person wanted to ride a merry-go-round, they would. At the same time that we reject the merry-go-round, we search for the thrill of an intense rollercoaster ride, but that doesn't mean we are suicidal—we want exciting but carefully maintained rollercoasters.

Given that we don't know a lot about the risks and dangers of particular BDSM practices, because no one will study or fund the research to answer those questions, the BDSM community must rely on its folk wisdom and anecdotes. But folk wisdom and anecdotes introduce quite a lot of variation, and, as a result, there are disagreements about how risky particular scenes are. A lack of knowledge makes community discussions around risk very difficult, but at least these discussions are farther along than the conversations found in medical and legal professions, or in mental healthcare.

The dynamic of shame within BDSM communities makes the discussion of risk difficult. People within organized BDSM communities can be extremely sensitive to anyone saying no, that's bad, or that's too much. At first blush, such a statement sounds like rejection and shame. It is on the surface, as Alan Downs puts it, invalidating. In a subculture that adores the image of the rebel, the outsider, the one who flirts with danger and is Mistress or Master of their own domain (or serving someone who is), being told by others in the community that a particular practice is too risky and should not be done is fraught with conflict and tension. The BDSM community strongly resists anyone who claims authority without proof or evidence of experience and, even then, the authority's expertise should be shared and not imposed. These dynamics make discussions that BDSM sometimes should not be practiced, that it is not healthy for some people in some situations, discussions that are often truncated or avoided because they are so difficult and emotionally hot.

Yet we maintain that it is within organized BDSM communities that deep insight and wisdom will arise, and having these conversations will strengthen the health and well-being of not only the entire community, but individual sexual outsiders as well.

Chapter Six

Power Is Hot

THE MISTRESS: A FANTASY

The man approached the house where he would lose his humanity. he both hungered and feared for what lay ahead, but the hunger was stronger than the fear.

The Mistress waited in Her space, Her realm, where She practiced and reenacted Her dark desires. While She enjoyed subjugating and using a man's body for Her physical pleasure and release, She craved something deeper. She wanted a man to appear, to approach Her, and give not just his body to Her will and pleasure, but also his mind, his heart, lust, passion, and the edges and undiscovered regions of his desire. She wanted to possess his very nature. The Mistress wanted someone who hungered to surrender to Her his social training, his niceties, his civilized face. She yearned for a man who hungered to let go of all shoulds *and* oughts—*self-control, control by society, control by others—and give that control to the Mistress.*

The man walked to the front door of the house and knew the door would be open for him. he knew that, once inside, his transformation would begin. he entered. The house was dark and quiet except for one candle lit in the foyer. he closed the door behind him and locked it, as instructed prior to his arrival. he turned and knelt, hands behind his back, and waited.

The Mistress descended the stairs. Dressed head to toe in leather, She carried a large, sharp knife. She stood in front of the kneeling man and examined him closely, first through sight only and then through touch. She lifted up the man's chin, grabbed the man's shirt, and began cutting into the shirt with Her knife.

The man did not move. The Mistress cut into the sleeves of the shirt, and finally ripped the rags off the man's upper body. She then put the knife to the throat of the man, and pressed the flat edge into the skin, to suggest the danger of the edge. She stood back.

"Stand."

The man stood up quickly. he put his hands behind his back again.

The Mistress stood closer. The knife in Her left hand, She grabbed the waistband of the pants and started cutting into them, making a sizable rip down the front. The Mistress walked around to the back, and started cutting again. The man could feel the steel of the knife, sometimes scraping his skin.

The Mistress ripped off the pants, and threw them down.

"Take those boots off." The man complied quickly. "And the socks."

The man stood naked.

The knife came closer to the chest, and the Mistress said, "you are Mine. you will give up all rights, responsibilities, and prerogatives of being a human. All birthrights, all expectations, all cares, all duties. you will give everything to Me."

She paused. "Do you do this willingly?"

"Yes, Mistress. i do."

The Mistress struck the face of the thing, to seal its fate. The hard slap made the thing see stars for a moment. It was pain, sealed in pain, and welcomed.

"Follow Me."

it followed, leaving behind the shreds of its clothing. Up the stairs, to the sanctuary.

The Mistress entered Her space, with Her toy following. She turned to face the object.

"I'm going to enjoy this, remaking it into an object of My pleasure and will."

The Mistress instructed the object to stand still for the next phase. The Mistress grabbed the clippers, after checking to make sure the water and shaving cream were in place and the straight razor was ready. She slowly ran the clippers over the entire body of the sex toy. "I'm removing anything that smacks of humanity—hair is for men and for animals, and you are a thing."

The clippers started on the chest. The caress and the scraping continued for some time. The clippers continued all the way down the front of the thighs and legs. The Mistress moved to the back, and again the clippers ran all over the object's body. Every inch was touched.

Then the Mistress told it to kneel. it immediately complied. The Mistress paused for a moment, breathed in deeply, and felt an immense surge of joy and power and lust. She then touched the clippers to the object's head. This part of the body would be Hers now.

The very visible head—She would mark it and remake it so that it would be obvious to the public that this thing was to be treated as an object. The clippers started moving over its head, the hair falling and slightly caressing the skin as it fell. Soon, the thing's head was just stubble. The Mistress stroked the head, checking and inspecting and enjoying the sensation.

The Mistress put the clippers back down and grabbed the shaving cream. She told the sex object to stand, and then started applying the cream. She took the straight razor and started shaving and scraping the skin, removing the stubble and stray hairs.

"Kneel," She ordered, and the object obeyed instantly.

The straight-edge razor was held in front of its eyes while the Mistress caressed and smoothed more shaving cream onto the head of the sex toy. The process of shaving and scraping the head lasted for several minutes, as the Mistress took Her time and enjoyed the process of stripping the object from all that animal hair. Soon, the head was smooth, with a thin shine. The Mistress put soothing ointment on the head to make it really shine—like marble and alabaster. Like metal. The Mistress told it to stand, and then She proceeded to use the straight edge on the rest of the object's body. Soon it stood completely hairless, the body gleaming.

The Mistress was proud.

The Mistress commanded, "Look into My eyes."

The sex toy did so, and suddenly felt a thrill of fear, surrender, passion, vulnerability, shame, and pride. "Let go. Let go of all of that. it will become a play thing, and a highly prized object of sexual art and a visual symbol of My Dominance. it is not responsible and it is not in control. it is doing just as I will, because there is no other will."

"it will stay here and rest, waiting until I want to use it again. That might be within the hour; it might be three days from now. it will wait and rest."

The Mistress's hand caressed the sex object, touching it lightly, admiring its performance and form and perfection.

"I am pleased."

The above fantasy was written by Chuck, a forty-year-old man, who shared it with his new female partner as part of their courting. Chuck works as a program evaluator for various state and federal programs and has been involved in the Kink/Fetish community in a large Midwestern city for about fifteen years. The new partner found it very erotic and the sharing of this fantasy was a significant moment in their growing intimate relationship. Chuck agreed to share it with us to illustrate some of the ideas we explore in this chapter.

One of the fundamental dynamics of BDSM sexualities is the eroticization of power. By *eroticization* we mean the way people can perceive power as having a sexually exciting dimension. They experience the expression of power as part of an enticing erotic allure and, generally, it is the power difference that creates the spark. Individuals can view someone as an object of lust and romance because they possess power. Although not as widely or openly discussed, it is also true that we can view someone as an object of lust and romance because they provide the illusion of being powerless or vulnerable. In a nonkinky way, we note Marilyn Monroe's goddess-like allure because she held a rare combination of sublime physical beauty coupled with an almost child-like naiveté and vulnerability. Although Sophia Loren, Elizabeth Taylor, and Brigitte Bardot were world-class beauties and film actresses during the 1950s and 1960s, they lacked the air of vulnerability that distinguished Marilyn Monroe. This juxtaposition made her a unique object of attraction. Power differentials can be linked to peoples' erotic imaginations.

The idea that powerlessness can be erotic and attractive is prevalent within the imaginations and practices of BDSM sexualities. This is an accepted fact within the BDSM subculture—after all, *bondage* is one of the key terms in the acronym *BDSM*. But away from that context and that culture, when we think of the eroticization of powerlessness, it comes close to the idea of sexual predators. People who get a sexual charge from someone else's vulnerability or powerlessness, and then act on that sexual impulse without negotiation, consent, or aftercare, are often confused with people who practice safe, sane, and consensual BDSM sexuality. The DSM-IV identifies *Sexual Sadism* as a mental disorder; our jails and prisons are holding numbers of men who are rapists, pedophiles, and sexual predators. Is the problem that humans eroticize power, or is the problem that people violate other people's boundaries and disregard their humanity during interactions with them? We would argue that the core mental health, forensic, and societal problem is the latter. We must recognize that some perfectly moral and healthy people also experience states of power and powerlessness as having an erotic dimension. An outright comparison of sexual predators to BDSM practitioners has not been done on a large scale, but several small-scale studies conducted with self-identified BDSM players find no significant level of mental disorders or mental health problems compared to the general population.[1] If sexual predators are suffering from a mental disorder or struggling with a mental illness, and the evidence shows that BDSM players are not, it then leaves a number of possibilities available. One possibility is that there will be an obvious difference in actual behavior and psychological motivation between criminal sexual predators diagnosed with Sexual Sadism and people involved in the BDSM communities. Another possibility is that the sexual aspects of the behavior do not have a clear relation to any mental illness and should not be a criterion for diagnosing mental illness at all.[2] Both of these possibilities do not support pathologizing the eroticization of power and powerlessness in itself.[3]

It is not just holding a position of power that can inspire others to view the holder as a sexual object; it also seems that having power often increases erotic behavior. Studies have found a connection between positions of power and the likelihood to approach and act, behaviors that also include an increase in sexual advances, flirtation, and an increase in interpreting others' behavior as indicating sexual interest.[4] Both as an element of attraction and as a motivational factor, power is often intertwined with sexual and erotic desires, for those into BDSM and even for those who are not.

Although the eroticization of power is an important component of BDSM sexualities, there are other equally important components, such as feeling particularly intense sensations or experiencing peak moments of consciousness. In these instances considerations of power differentials as erotic are secondary themes. Not all BDSM sexuality is about power, but playing with power is a notable common characteristic among people participating in the subculture. In fact, some have argued that power exchange and what we call the eroticization of power may be more of an accurate description of what BDSM is, rather than a definition that focuses on pain or aggression.

Esther Perel, in her book *Mating in Captivity*, discusses the need for space and differentiation in creating and sustaining erotic charges between couples. Eros moves us, and it moves us toward the Unknown Other—that is the function of erotic desire, its basic nature. When two people are too close to each other psychologically, there is no distance to transverse, no gap to move across, and the basic dynamic of the erotic impulse is frustrated or made much more difficult to sustain. Perel notes that people who have sustained long-lasting erotic partnerships approach each other as if their partner is an undiscovered country, even after years of living together.

The use and exchange of power is one of the many ways that couples have created the psychological distance and relational mystery that are necessary for Eros. Perel discusses several cases where couples have used BDSM scenes and power exchanges to keep the erotic alive in their long-term relationships. We have also witnessed couples, triads, and other relationship configurations using BDSM powerplay as an important element in maintaining long-term relationships.

We'll explore several kinds of kink to illustrate the dynamics of playing with power: the 24/7 Dominant/submissive relationship; voyeurism/exhibitionism as scenes or aspects of scenes; impact play; raunch (play with bodily fluids and products, like sweat, saliva, urine, and excrement); and age play or age regression. In presenting these five examples, we demonstrate the eroticization of power as a basic underlying dynamic spanning many different expressions of kink.

While looking at these examples, we don't wish to give the impression that these particular kinks are common or somehow the markers of "real" kinky people, or that all kinky people participate in these activities. In fact, we'll never be able to define *kink* absolutely because it's about the eroticism of power and, since power is fluid and works at several levels simultaneously, it is so complex that its experience is essentially unique to each person.

Power differences occur in so many places in our lives, allowing for a range of influential experiences during the formation of our sexuality, that any description for one person will not fit another. Rather than get hung up on what it looks like or what the behavior is, we want to go underneath and explore some of the psychological dynamics and the meanings of *kink*. With that in mind, kink, like all sexuality, is "polymorphously perverse" (thank you, Dr. Freud); it is important to know that you're not alone, even though your particular kink may be very rare and unusual.

For example, a close friend of one of the authors is incredibly sexually aroused by the sound and visualization of blowing up balloons—the bigger, more beautiful, and more intricate the balloon the better. Popping them can bring on an orgasm. "My fetish makes birthday parties and big restaurant celebrations a bit of a challenge," Keith laughs. "It's really fun to blow up balloons, roll around with them, feel their sensation against my body, and finally hear that POP! I enjoy it alone, but with a friend or play partner it's beyond!"

There are few descriptive studies that have attempted to find out how common or rare certain practices are among people who identify as kinky or into BDSM. Moser and Levitt conducted a survey of 178 men and women who affirmed that they define part of their sexuality as S/M.[5] They found that a majority had engaged in impact play (spanking, 82 percent; whipping, 65 percent); a portion had engaged in age-regression roleplay (32 percent teacher-student scene; 20 percent guardian-child scene); and some had experience with raunch play (44 percent watersports; 12.5 percent scat play; watersports refers to erotic play with urine and scat play refers to erotic play with feces). Breslow, Evans, and Langley conducted a survey of 182 individuals contacted through an S/M-oriented magazine, and found that 32 percent had an interest in watersports, 17 percent had an interest in toilet activities, 80 percent had an interest in spanking, and 45 percent in whipping.[6] Jennifer Rehor in a survey of 1,361 women contacted through BDSM community organizations found that 94 percent of the women respondents had experience with spanking, 76 percent with flogging; 36 percent had experience with watersports, 6 percent with scat play; 36 percent had some experience with age-regression roleplay; and 50 percent had some experience with cybersex, which we would qualify as a form of exhibitionism/voyeurism, if not in the usual meaning of the terms. Fifty-six percent had some experience with exhibitionism in the usual meaning of the term, and for many this traditional exhibitionism was an expression of a power dynamic, in that the exhibitionism was part of obeying an order to display given by their Dominant or Domme.[7]

Let's take a look at these five practices through the lens of playing with power dynamics.

The 24/7 Relationship

> Lydia on power: "The first time I realized I had it, I wanted to give it up. In my career, I'm a rockstar, at the very top of my game. In the playroom, I want anything but THAT."

> Nathan on power: "I feel like I've never had power, so when I get to pretend I do, my world opens up. Maybe someday I'll feel like I actually have it. For real."

The 24/7 relationship is consciously structured and organized around a power exchange, one person having authority over another that extends beyond the time boundaries of a specific scene or encounter. A Dominant or submissive role is maintained not only for a few hours in the dungeon or playspace, but also in the rest of the home and in other places beyond the home. The Dominant/submissive 24/7 relationship may have similar roles and identities as other BDSM relationships that are not 24/7 (Mistress/slave, Sir/boy, Dom/sub, Daddy/girl), but the significant difference is the extent of the time window of the power exchange and, sometimes, the depth of the power exchange.

The 24/7 relationship is often couched in terms of *collaring* or *ownership*. The imagery of slavery, or owning an animal or object, is often used to signify the power-based relationship. A collar signifies that someone is owned or claimed, that they belong to a Domme or Dominant. Sometimes the Dom will carry a key to signify their relationship to the collared. Within the larger BDSM subculture and in BDSM community spaces people recognize and support the ongoing power-based relationship by acknowledging a set of protocols and rituals that uphold the boundaries of that 24/7 relationship. For example, people will know to refrain from touching a submissive's chain or leather collar.

The extension of the power exchange beyond a specific scene or particular place is challenging to create and often challenging to understand.

In coming to understand 24/7 relationships specifically, and BDSM in general, the overarching concept of *orientation* can be of help. Many people within BDSM communities discuss BDSM as an orientation, using ideas and constructs similar to that of sexual orientation as we normally use the term. In our own research and clinical practice, we refer to this concept as *erotic orientation* to distinguish it from sexual orientation—an orientation toward erotic power exchange. We conceptualize this as a dimension, similar to Kinsey's scale of heterosexual–homosexual behaviors or feelings. One person may be very oriented to erotic power exchange, a "6", while someone else may not be oriented to erotic power exchange at all, a "0." We imagine that this might be distributed normally in the general population, with most people dispersed throughout the middle and fewer people at the extremes.

People who engage in 24/7 power-structured relationships are at one extreme of this type of proposed orientation scale.

Many people, or perhaps all, who engage in 24/7 relationships have a strong orientation to power exchange. "It's like trying to explain being gay," according to a member of the BDSM community in a relatively new 24/7 relationship. Justin, an investment broker near the Great Lakes, discussed his entry into a Master/slave relationship as an occurrence similar to "coming home," knowing it was the right thing, but being scared of making the significant decision to try a 24/7 relationship, knowing that "everything will shift." He explained his "difficulty in walking through that door." His thoughts, words, and feelings around the topic of getting into a 24/7 relationship were exactly like those of coming out.

Justin is not the only one who has experienced this. "It's like being gay" provides family members, partners, and friends with a key metaphor in relating to the kinky person. In these situations, it is not surprising to come across the same dynamics that someone who is bisexual, gay, lesbian, or transgender will have in acknowledging this aspect of themselves: anxiety about the process of coming out to family, friends, and associates, wrestling with internalized homophobia or transphobia, and managing the stress of being marginalized as a sexual minority. The same psychological dynamics and dilemmas apply for kinky people who have made this aspect of their sexuality more central to their daily lives and identities: the anxiety about coming out, wrestling with internalized "kink-phobia," and the stress of being marginalized or erased as a sexual minority. The skills required to relate to LGBT family members or LGBT communities are transferable, in many ways, to work with kinky family members or BDSM communities.

In addition to the set of sexual minority concerns that come up in providing mental healthcare in our work, there are two other sets of issues and concerns that we encounter frequently: those related to being in any type of relationship, and those related to the specific contours and characteristics of 24/7 Dominant/submissive relationships.

Any kind of relationship involves issues of communication, trust, and intimacy. Those who live 24/7 relationships exhibit the same issues in ways that are just like any other intimate relationship. Because intimate relationships involve the intertwining of attachment and security needs, erotic desires and needs, and friendship dynamics—three very different sets of needs and motivations—it is not surprising that the issues of communication, trust, and intimacy are common. The three sets of needs and motivations are sometimes in tension with each other. The need for safety and close bonding works at odds with the mystery and distance that enhances erotic desires. The need for intimacy requires a vulnerable exchange between two peers relating on equal footing, but this becomes more difficult when one person is more concerned with protecting the self from perceived threats and dangers—and that protection means withholding intimacy and disclosure. Adding to the mix a power-structured relationship might enhance some of these needs, but make other needs trickier to meet, but a 24/7 dynamic doesn't fundamentally change the complex set of needs people bring to all intimate relationships.

The second set of concerns are the ones particular to maintaining a 24/7 power-structured relationship. In order to maintain a power exchange, both parties make different but complementary promises. Charlie, who is a submissive to Frank, tells us: "I promise to refuse Him nothing and He promises to never send me away." Sophia, who is submissive to Adam, promises to give her life to Adam, and Adam promises to take care of Sophia. The promises are not the same, but their difference allows for the two people to maintain a polarity in power. By promising and committing to portray different roles, to be held to different standards for each other, but still promising to be steadfast and to place the other as important, the 24/7 vows are in some ways similar to vows from earlier times or from other cultures. These vows are in some ways noticeably different from the twenty-first-century Western vows that emphasize both partners making the same exact promises as signs of equality between independent, autonomous selves.

Sophia discusses how one tricky sticking point occurs when her plans, desires, and goals are in conflict with her Master's schedule, plans, and desires—and the difficulty of adhering to her promise to submit her intentions and behavior to His authority, while simultaneously acknowledging that she always has the ability to disobey to take care of her core needs. One of her core needs is to experience the joy of service. "I can stop this at any second if I want. I have more control than Adam does, around that boundary. But this service is joy, not fear. It is my will to give my life to Adam. Service brings me joy."

Charlie also discusses the joy he experiences in helping Frank, emphasizing that in moments of service he does not experience any distress or anxiety. It has taken Charlie a while to accept that it is okay for him to want what Frank wants.

A therapist, family member, or friend must confront how he or she views complementary promises, rather than promises that are the same exact promises exchanged between two people.

Probably the biggest hurdle for providing competent care to people in 24/7 relationships is how standard or traditional therapy has embodied the Western cultural value placed on the independent self, or individualism, a cultural value that reflects a particular Western European Enlightenment theory of self, health, and well-being. Concepts like codependency and enmeshment can be used inappropriately to denigrate collectivism and interdependence as a cultural value. These clashing values show up again and again in the history of psychology and therapy—in the history of how some traditional Western psychological theories were biased against women's experiences because the theories viewed interdependence and the relational self as being psychologically immature. Therefore women, socialized to value relationships and family over their individual desires and needs, were assessed as psychologically immature compared to men. Multicultural counseling theory and practice often notes how mismatches in values and miscommunications occur between individualistic versus collectivistic orientations. The mismatch leads to situations where therapists, often from white Western European middle-class backgrounds, would misdiagnose, overdiagnose, or underdiagnose patients from different cultural backgrounds. Some client cultural backgrounds do not hold an independent self or individualism as a central part of their worldview. Is having a more interdependent self inherently more pathogenic, generating illness and disorders? Are people who place loyalty to their families or to their in-group above their own independent goals psychologically immature? We are hard-pressed to point to any evidence that clearly supports a pathologizing viewpoint on collectivistic or interdependent selves.

We propose that 24/7 Dominant/submissive relationships can be viewed through this lens. What if submissives operate with an interdependent self and a relational worldview? What if Dominants also value the connections that define their relationships to others, more than acting in narcissistic or egocentric ways reflecting individualism? Some Dominants discuss how much effort they pour into making space and opportunities for their submissives to serve them. This is not selfish or egotistical. It is possible that there is a lot of similarity between a healthy 24/7 relationship and intimate domestic relationships that occur between adults in other cultures. Just as a culturally competent therapist must raise the question of whether they are working under an assumption that an interdependent self is always unhealthy, so too must a culturally competent therapist raise the question of whether a Dominant/submissive relationship is always unhealthy simply because it is different than the mainstream culture that values individualism, egalitarianism, and an independent self.

Twenty-four/seven total power exchanges are an intense expression of eroticizing power differentials. There are men and women who find it more natural to relate in ways that are complementary rather than egalitarian, emphasizing differences in roles to create a polarity that allows for the exchange of power. They appear to do so because their experience of erotic desire is greatly charged by power differences.

Voyeurism and Exhibitionism: The Power of the Look

We've talked with people who get an erotic thrill out of being watched and others by watching and observing, particularly in more intimate activities and settings. In his *Dark Eros: The Imagination of Sadism*, Thomas Moore provides a psychotherapist's interpretation of the writings of the Marquis de

Sade. One of the major themes in Sade's writings involves the libertines, who are in positions of power, often examining, inspecting, and objectifying the people they find sexually attractive. Moore notes that Sade capitalizes on the inherent power differential between the viewer and the viewed to comment on the nature of society and sexuality, and—in particular—the world's aggression and cruelty toward the vulnerable and innocent. There are power dynamics inherent in observing, inspecting, and viewing. When looking specifically at the act of inspection, the one who inspects another holds a position of power and control, while the subject of inspection is in a position of powerlessness. Being open, vulnerable, and seen—to be the object of someone else's viewing—is a masochistic act, according to Moore's reading of Sade's imagination, while observing, inspecting, and viewing another is an act of sadism, the taking of an aggressive stance toward another.

Certain BDSM submissives get an erotic charge out of being in a powerless position, and being viewed, inspected, or put on display is a visceral, complete way of inhabiting that submissive role. They explain that part of the thrill is inspiring a heightened level of desire in others. The displayed has the power to drive the viewer into ecstasy. At first glance, the inspected or viewed individual may appear to be in a position of complete powerlessness but, on closer analysis, they are very much in control and in possession of power. This dialectic of power and powerlessness is crucial to understanding why someone would want to be objectified in a scene or encounter.

Because the act of inspection involves viewing, it is not difficult to recognize the place of theatrical spectacle in our sexuality. It is not solely inspection, but the broader act of watching that is wrought with erotic thrill. The emotional and psychological distance between the inspector and the inspected, the audience and the performer, is a source of dramatic or erotic tension. That tension is part of the excitement phase of sexual arousal. People use both the act of watching and the act of showing off as a way to build higher and increased levels of desire.

In the words of William Shakespeare, "All the world's a stage, and all the men and women merely players." The social commentary of the illustrious Jaques in *As You Like It* applies to so much in life. The world, and our place in it, is an act of theater—a series of psychodramas enacted in communion with others in various settings and with a variety of props. Life is theater and we are not only the players, but the audience as well. Rare are the moments when we are not watching someone, even unconsciously, and sometimes that someone is ourselves. We constantly see, absorb, and often evaluate even the smallest things that cross our path. Consequently, we are also seen and these states of seeing and being seen can often have an erotic component.

BDSM communities take the art of theatricality to new levels. Costumes such as a military uniform, a tightly cinched corset, a pair of leather chaps, or a wrestling singlet all evoke a different erotic mood. Add to these costumes a corresponding prop—a riding crop, an ostrich feather, a motorcycle, or a wrestling mat—and you've got theater of the sexy. Though playful and exponentially erotic, we need to underscore that this theatricality in no way detracts from or falsifies the core identities that many community members would argue, with good reason, are not an act but an orientation central to their core self-understanding.

People in the BDSM communities understand the power dynamic of exhibitionism and voyeurism very well. Many major cities have public dungeons, parties, or gathering places where BDSM scenes can be enacted in the presence of others. Not every kinky person enjoys this kind of public scene, but many do. There is an erotic thrill to watching others, and in being on display for others to view. Public play enhances the power exchange.

For example, some cities have leather/kink street fairs, and perhaps the granddaddy of them all is the Folsom Street Fair in San Francisco every September. People fly from all over the globe look at others, and to be on the "stage" of the street so others can look at them, and Folsom is a "stage" that draws 300,000 to 450,000 attendees. It is a ritual that celebrates exhibitionism and voyeurism.

The public display that is central to community events like play parties, leather/kink street fairs, or large gatherings of kinky players can also be an expression of power at both community and individual levels. Hence, there is a confluence of community pride and erotic dynamics, as community pride becomes intertwined with the power dynamics of exhibitionism and voyeurism. The personal becomes the political, and the political penetrates the personal realm. The flamboyant display, the outrageous fetish gear, and the public display of BDSM skill all generate an erotic current for both the exhibitionist and the audience. Voyeurism and exhibitionism also embody and recreate the BDSM community's value of overt sexuality. Community empowerment also connects to people's individual erotic lives by creating spaces, events, and opportunities for sexually kinky people to find, and connect with, each other. Pride is expressed through display and public performance, and that empowerment is a critical element in overcoming an oppressive invisibility and marginalization.

There is a shadow side to this recurrent theme of exhibitionism and voyeurism in BDSM sexualities and communities. We can't begin to count the number of times a patient has said, "I just want to be seen!" or, "I'm so afraid to be seen!" The Shadow side of display, inspection, and "show" is shame. Shame arises out of a vulnerable exposure to another's rejecting glare and gives rise to a need to hide.

There are at least three ways in which shame plays a role in exhibitionism or voyeurism: healing from shame, the thrill of shame, and reaction formation. Many people find that pushing through shame and being able to put themselves out on display or in front of an audience is a healing act. Others find that being "forced" to exhibit themselves, or being exposed by the look of a voyeur, raises intense feelings of shame. This feeling of exposure and vulnerability stirs up a fight-or-flight response, which in turn releases endorphins and a cascade of other hormones. Neurological studies have found that social pain (like shame and humiliation) is processed in the brain using the same circuitry as physical pain, and we know that the body's counteraction to physical pain is the release of pain-modulating or pain-relieving hormones and neurotransmitters. Just as a runner or weightlifter might push their bodies into experiences of "pain" in order to grow, in order to experience the reward of the physical rush and pleasure on the other side of that exertion, people sometimes also push their minds and spirits into experiences of vulnerability, shame, or exposure in order to grow and to feel the rush of feelings that counteract the social pain. Yes, some of us look at runners and say to ourselves, "That's just crazy! Why do that to yourself?" Similarly, some of us might look at kinky people and say the same thing, but the underlying dynamic is similar to other instances where people push or challenge themselves, or seem to move toward uncomfortable situations with the goal of growth or transcendence.

While there might be consciously healing intentions behind exhibitionism and voyeurism, or intentions to feel the rush of endorphins in response to feelings of shame, there may also be attempts to convince ourselves that we don't feel shame about our sexuality when, in fact, we still hold deep reservoirs of embarrassment and shame inside. Exhibitionism or voyeurism can mask and distract from shame without really addressing it. Getting to the point that one can celebrate (exhibit) and have pride in one's sexual identity doesn't mean that all shame and internalized rejection have been resolved.

People in BDSM communities might ask themselves, "How can I possibly have shame about being a submissive or Dominatrix when I'm out here in the middle of a street fair, convention, or leather event? Isn't that proof enough that I don't?" Questions like these and the assertion that we are not acting in a shame-based way might relieve a person of the noxious burden of feeling any shame in that moment.

Shame is deeply connected to power, to experiences of powerlessness or the exertion of power to enforce one's rules or expectations, as when we shame others. Because shame is about "being seen" and being exposed, it is not surprising that exhibitionism and voyeurism are prominent erotic themes in BDSM sexuality and central to some prominent events within BDSM communities.

Impact Play

Spanking, paddling, caning, flogging, whipping—these are the just some of the techniques that involve impact to the body. Impact play can be about physical sensation-seeking, it can be about catharsis or healing, or it can be about the expression and exertion of power between people. When impact play is about power, it involves an asymmetrical relation: I can touch you, but you cannot touch me. It can also be about endurance, a chance to prove your worth and utility to the Dom or Mistress. This may involve themes of initiation, meeting a challenge, and demonstrating personal power and worthiness by successfully passing through the rigors of the scene. Often impact play is about "breaking the will" of the submissive, which would be the ultimate powerplay.

Geoff Mains, in his classic *Urban Aboriginals*, discusses the use of impact play like whipping and flogging as a ritual not very different from other tribal rituals of initiation. He also discusses the symbolic aspects of the instruments of impact play, such as a strap or paddle, and how these become connected to roles of dominance. In a section entitled "Pain as Authority," Mains comments on how society at large uses involuntary pain and punishment for social control and thus the maintenance of a social dominance hierarchy. Grounded in our evolutionary makeup as social primates, the initiation rituals across many human societies are expressions of the group's authority over the individual and their recognition and sanction of a significant movement from one social category to another (from child to adult, from boy to man, from girl to woman, from an "average" person to a warrior or leader). The inhabitants of the BDSM world appropriated this basic stance and have turned it into play, intertwining it with Eros, and often using "pain as initiation" as a theme for particular scenes. People deeply involved in the BDSM communities also use rituals of initiation that function to acknowledge a change in social standing and social category within the BDSM subculture.

Mains also discusses the use of impact play as spiritual catharsis, a theme also found in many cultures and societies. Pain from impact becomes a surrender to authority, to divine authority, or an act of sacrifice to demonstrate one's deep commitment to a spiritual ideal or authority. That surrender to an authority figure also connects one to that source of power and authority. It encourages a deep connection to the group, by affirming one's place in a social dominance hierarchy—and also one's place in a spiritual hierarchy, where there are beings or energies more powerful than the individual.

One other expression of impact play as it relates to power is the use of it to break a person's will. Here, the scene becomes a dramatic enactment of resistance and overcoming that resistance. To whip or flog someone into submission means to have the ability to keep inflicting intense sensation until the bottom no longer has the wherewithal to defend or act against the Top. Going from resistance to compliance is a journey that creates an intense vulnerability on the part of the bottom, and being able to lead a bottom on that journey becomes an incredible experience of power and ability for the Top.

Impact play is the most visible sign that easily allows people unfamiliar with BDSM sexualities to see this kind of powerplay as violence and aggression, and therefore label it as antisocial, dangerous, and sick. Given that, we must take a moment to discuss how violence and aggression are viewed.

Violence is often used interchangeably with *aggression*, yet some would hold that *violence* involves physical force with the intent of gaining dominance over another person or persons,[8] while *aggression* can involve force for instrumental reasons as well as hostile intentions and not have anything to do with dominance. Instrumental aggression is when we use force to gain a goal that is secondary to the act, as when we break a window to get out of a burning building or when a lioness hunts a gazelle to feed her cubs. Surgeons often cut in order to heal; parents often enforce a rule through punishment or the removal of privileges for the health and well-being of a child, against the wishes of the child. In these cases, we recognize the "good" intention behind the "aggressive" or "dominating/violent" act. Hostile aggression is when we use force to intentionally inflict pain or harm on another in order to make them suffer, and the forceful act is the primary means to the goal. Research on aggression in childhood and adolescence will often make a distinction between physical aggression and nonphysical aggression (which can be verbal, such as insulting someone, or relational, as when we gossip about someone in order to turn others against them). The variety of ways in which violence and aggression are defined for the purposes of scientific study illuminates how difficult it is to categorize specific actions as aggressive or violent. Even something like a slap to the face can have several meanings, interpretations, and can be an expression of care (like when trying to get the attention of a hysterical person to calm them down and help them) or an expression of harm. BDSM clearly raises questions about what counts as violence.

We use the definition of *violence* and *aggression* as "crossing another person's boundaries against their will," whether that boundary is their actual skin, or their psychological self-boundary, a boundary that might extend beyond their physical skin to include their possessions, their interpersonal space, or even their concept of self. Because these acts of force are often judged by the person's intentions, what counts as violence is often a matter of the viewpoint of the person making the judgment or assessment.[9] Perhaps BDSM always involves violence and aggression, but the study of forceful actions pushes us to make a distinction between aggression for pro-social ends and aggression for antisocial ends. Impact play can leave marks, bruises, cuts, and sometimes blood and tears. It is the most concrete form of crossing another person's boundary. But the power exchange is done voluntarily. It is negotiated and consensually co-created, and crossing that boundary leads to increased trust, bonding, and connection for some BDSM players. It can be a means to spiritual catharsis or creating a power exchange that heightens sexual excitement and intimacy. We must ask ourselves, in light of the experience of sexual outsiders: are violence and aggression always bad, dangerous, or pathological? If we determine that aggression is always bad, we must not only wonder about people into BDSM but also critically inquire about policing, acts of war, and playing sports, and their place and value in society, since all of these also use violence and aggression against peoples' bodies as a means to an end.

Our own particular take on this question is that the kind of violence or aggression that is morally reprehensible is the violence or aggression that is not consensual, that is involuntary. While recognizing that society may use this dubious means to further a greater good, we question whether that makes it even permissible. Clearly, there are examples and ideas of how to enact social control and order without the use of violence or aggression. The long tradition of nonviolent political protest and the use of community patrols that protect people without tools of violence are examples of enacting social control and order without the use of violence and aggression. But would that line, the line created by voice, consent, and the individual's right to self-determination, leave room for sports, initiation rituals, BDSM, or the proper use of aggression? We think so.

Edge Play: Raunch and Age Regression

The last two types of scenes we'll explore are sometimes labeled as *edge play* in the BDSM communities.

What is edge play?

The primary meaning, as used by many people within BDSM communities, is play that is either physically risky and/or intensely socially taboo. This would include scenes that involve breath control or choking, scenes that involve reenactments of power differentials based on race (called race play), play with knives and cutting or piercing with needles (bloodsports), scenes involving bodily excrement, and roleplays that involve age regression. The secondary meaning of edge play defines it as play that explores, pushes, and stretches a person's limits, emotionally and physically, regardless of the exact toys, tools, or script used. In this secondary meaning, one person's edge is another person's familiar comfort zone. Because people's experience levels and their likes and dislikes differ, edge play will vary from one person to the next. The case of Darren and Alicia, which we discussed in chapter 4, is an example of this second meaning of edge play—the actual physical aspects of the scene were not very physically risky or crossing a strongly held social taboo, but the edge was much more personal and psychological.

Edge play is controversial, even within BDSM communities. These are activities that tend to be debated hotly, or that often encounter a noticeable squick response among many kinky people. Playing on the edge of social taboos, in particular, is controversial because it taps into an almost-universal fear of going too far, or accesses the shame we have internalized, a shame that socializes us to behave in ways that are socially sanctioned as good or appropriate.

People who play on the edge are playing with fire and the deep unknown. While the thrill of transgressing a taboo can lead to an experience of freedom from social bonds that don't quite fit, there is also a heightened risk of going too far and hurting, perhaps even harming. Playing with fire means, however, that we learn more about the very nature of fire, how it can be used for good as well as for evil. Exploring the edges benefits the entire group, as long as the explorer returns to the fold to share their newfound knowledge and relate their experience to those who choose not to venture out to the edges.

Some forms of raunch play and age regression do have greater chances of risk, physically or psychologically. They approach and explore very powerful forces within peoples' psyches. As we continue our exploration into the power dynamics that attract people to BDSM, we recognize that, while the manifestations of these dynamics are edgy and taboo, they lie on the same continuum of powerplay as 24/7 relationships, voyeurism and exhibitionism, and impact play. Understanding the erotic nature of powerplay can give friends, family members, mental-health professionals, and society a way to better understand this form of human sexuality.

Raunch Play

"Okay, that's gross."

Gross.

We probably first heard the word somewhere on that universal grammar school playground. Little Johnnie MacIntyre was picking his nose. Someone pointed and said, "Ew, that's gross," and poor little Johnnie cried his eyes out in shame and went through life terrified to ever touch his nose again.

And that was the end of the conversation about Johnnie MacIntyre and his rhinitis. Playing the gross card, as we've come to call it, even as adults, passes an immediate sentence on the topic or action at hand, and the passing of that sentence aborts the conversation or action in the name of its own "grossness."

There are a number of things we, individually or as a societal collective, find gross, but that doesn't mean the world stops talking about them.

There are a number of things we, individually or as a societal collective, find gross, but that doesn't mean the world stops talking about them. Using "it's gross," is an acceptable, if blunt, expression of opinion but it cannot become an allowable manipulation that shuts down dialogue or something that censors. I saw a particularly gross tie on a man riding the subway this morning. I may (and really did) find it gross, but that doesn't give me the right to ask him to remove it. Frankly, it may even be rude to mention my opinion. But rudeness doesn't necessarily deter the kids on the playground or the adults they grow up to become.

In naming this section "Raunch Play," we need to note that, though the terms *raunch* or *raunchy* are often used in a judgmental or pejorative way, we are using them because communities that play with sweat, saliva, urine, and excrement have reclaimed these words and use them as an affirming name for their identities and play. We've seen similar language reclamations by sexual, gender, racial, and ethnic minorities who've adopted the negative slurs once (and sometimes still) applied to them and employed them in a positive or empowering way.

> I'm a pig, and I identify that way. I'm proud of it. Pigs are cute. So am I. I do the nastiest things sexually and I'm proud of that. I go against the grain, not because I want to throw it into people's faces but because it's who I am.
>
> —Tommy, thirty-four-year-old paralegal and pig (Sacramento, CA)

The word *scat* is derived from the ancient Greek word for dung or excrement. In the context of this discussion, however, *scat* refers to sexual play involving excrement.

Scat play encompasses an array of sexual activities. Some scat players are only into the visual aspects, such as watching someone excrete or looking at an unflushed toilet. Many are into smearing excrement on their bodies. And some like to lick or eat fecal matter. For many scat aficionados some combination of these activities is most erotic.

Psychologically, it is multifaceted as well. For some, scat play is an extremely intimate exchange. For others it serves as the climax of a heavy BDSM or humiliation scene with a focus on power. It can be incorporated with diaper play and age play. If it has to do with the intersection of excrement and sex, it's called scat play.

We begin with a story told to us by Kevin, a gay leatherboy turned Leatherman who admits that he's "consistently surprised by what I'll try if I feel connected to the power of the man I'm with." Kevin is a phlebotomist from San Diego, California.

If you'd told me even a year before that I would be lying face up in a shower receiving scat from my partner and Master in my impatient open mouth, I would have left the room. Scat was gross to me. It had a squick factor that was off any measurable scale. Watersports brought up a similar sense of revulsion, but less so. My squick factor for piss play was probably measurable on some scale. Somewhere.

So how did I end up on that particular shower floor in rural Massachusetts, submissive and hungry for a new experience, pleasuring my Sir so passionately He was making sounds I'd never heard before from any human or animal?

To begin with, you have to understand His smell. From the moment I met Him, I was hit with two powerful sensations: the sight of His incredibly blue eyes and His overwhelming scent. I don't know if it was pheromones, energy, or what, but whenever He came into my olfactory range, I would involuntarily leak sticky strings of precum into the white Calvin Klein briefs I favored. Boys, I thought, always wore white briefs. Sexy, cool, grown-up underwear was for adult men—real men. At twenty-eight, I fantasized and placed myself somewhere around age seventeen—a high-school boy with a raging sex drive. Good grades, good manners, and preppy clothes by day. Tight Levis, torn shirt, and tied over a motorcycle prone for whatever my Sir wanted by night. The juxtaposition was naughty and taboo, and the fantasy was my first expression of age play, something that excited me more than I ever expected. Playing younger than my natural age was thrilling to me.

I had told my Sir on numerous occasions that my holes were His to do with and use as He pleased. My mouth and anus were His. I knew He wouldn't hesitate to use me. I was (still) a virgin and it was remarkably uncomfortable to breathe through the first few times He put Himself inside me, "making you Mine," He would say.

He loved me very much, and though He tested and expanded my limits, He never asked me to do anything that pushed me too far. He spoke often about His desire for me to kneel before Him, take His cock in my mouth, and rather than suck it, to just let it rest there while He urinated in my mouth. Though I always felt a tingle in my crotch when He spoke of this desire, my own socially programmed shame around bodily fluids trumped. "When you're ready," He said, those blue eyes full of love and a crystal-clear knowledge of His full control over me. "And if you never are, I still—and always will—love you."

A boy couldn't have asked for a better Man to be his first Master, the first consistent guide through the more advanced levels of erotic powerplay, submission, and vulnerability. He was a Dad to my son, a Coach to my jock, a Sir to my boy, and a Master to the slave I knew would never be a true identity, but a role I could explore safely with Him.

Throughout my training under Him, His unique smell was consistent. I can't call it a scent, as the word barely conveys the power His smell had over me. I'd experienced some light bondage, some spanking, and some roleplays previously—ever since I came out into the gay male Leather community when I was twenty-three. Sir took me further. It was under His lash that I first experienced the sensation of a four-foot single tail cracking against my back. So high was His level of skill, He could flick that whip so gracefully I felt butterfly kisses on my back. In the next stroke, He could leave a welt that lasted a week. Before my service to Him, I had been spanked, but it was He who made me buy a special black leather belt that He always wore when we were together. He was the first Man to beat my bottom until my flesh opened. I had marks for a week and wore a jockstrap to the gym every day so that when I changed the other men could see the marks He left on my bottom. That is how proud I was of them. Sure, I'd been tied up before, but Sir was the first to tie me down to complete immobility. He never told me what He was going to do to me once I was tied down, but that was part of the thrill. I was committed to try almost anything with Him, because I genuinely loved Him and trusted Him beyond any question. He once offered me a safeword, and for the only time in my life then or since, I refused it. My instincts told me that, with Him, I would never need one. And I never did.

We were at a play party in the Mendocino countryside about a year and a half into our relationship. Sir had restrained me publicly and worked my back and bottom over with His belt, His whip, and His flogger for the better part of two hours. During the scene, Sir never failed to come around to me, crook His finger under my chin, instruct me to meet His gaze, and ask me how I was doing—physically and emotionally—every ten to fifteen minutes. During one of these check-ins, high on the endorphins of a long impact session, I told Him that I needed to pee. He smiled and told me that He did too. He released me from my bondage and we walked together, Him fully dressed and me fully naked, my back and butt an even shade of pulsating bright red, to one of the more remote bathrooms in the playspace.

He stood behind me, holding my penis in His hand while I urinated. This was always His practice and I never questioned it. When I was relieved, He shook it free of any residual droplets and turned me to face Him. The smell and the eyes, not to mention my absolute adoration of Him intoxicated me. Something inside of me knew it was time. I'll never know if it was my idea or His or some combination of the two, but I found myself kneeling on the cold tiles before Him.

"Are you sure, son?" He asked.

"Yes, Sir. I am."

He unbuckled the belt, popped the button of His jeans and lowered His zipper. He placed His erection in my waiting, open mouth and let it sit on my tongue until His hardness abated. I did everything I could to remain orally still and not stimulate Him. I knew He could not pee with a hard-on. Sir was big. Even soft, He filled my mouth. I felt His cock lay against my tongue, my nose and mouth buried in His pubic hair, one of my particularly favorite sources of His amazing smell. I heard Him groan lightly and I felt wetness and warmth against my tongue. Sir was pissing in my mouth. It didn't taste like I imagined it would. It was slightly sour and very warm. We'd been playing for awhile out in the playroom and Sir must have really needed to pee. For what felt like five or six minutes, the stream was relentless, spraying into my mouth and down my throat. I swallowed every drop and (surprising myself) never gagged once. Sir's hand gently grasping the back of my neck was a source of comfort and support. When He was done, my belly was full of His piss and I was so hard I thought my skin would tear. He laughingly told me later that He practically had to pry my mouth off His cock. Bellyful of piss or not, I clearly wanted more. From that day forward, Sir never used a urinal again. I was His urinal, and I found myself looking forward to it. I loved every moment of that first session of being Sir's piss boy. I surprised myself. I also found myself masturbating about that scene for years afterward. Actually, I still do.

The intimacy, vulnerability, and submission of accepting a Man's bodily fluids had long been a fantasy of mine, but in the era of HIV, I knew that was something that would need to remain in the realm of my dreams. Piss was relatively safe, being sterile. After years of fantasizing about it, I had finally accepted another Man's fluids into my body. The fact that it was Sir only made it better. I had never felt more submissive, intimate, vulnerable, and connected with Him than I did in that moment.

About a year later Sir and I were at His weekend house in Massachusetts. This was one of our erotic escapes when I would visit the East Coast. Sir liked to have sex and beat me every day, which was more than I desired, but pleasing Him and obeying Him was integrally more important than my wants and needs. Some people might say that's not healthy. For me, it was a relief. I was very driven, strong, on point, and successful in all aspects of my life. In my relationship with Sir I didn't have to do or be that. I could let go and be soft, relaxed, and not in control. I could be a boy and let Him be the Man, and I trusted Him enough that I could allow myself to be that boy. Actually, those moments of letting go of my neurotic ambitious Man-self with Sir may have helped my mental and spiritual health in the long run.

Even though Sir whipped me, tied me up, and used my mouth as a urinal, we had very traditional and standard sex too. That afternoon I was massaging and kissing His backside, finally flicking my tongue across His anus. Sir was a strict Top and had never been a bottom but He loved it when I rimmed Him and I did it as often as He would allow me because I could be so close to one of His most visceral scents—one of many that drove me to extreme arousal. I enjoyed using my mouth and tongue to serve, probe, and experience Sir. I would often lose track of time during these session, which I did that afternoon.

Sir's muscles were very relaxed and my tongue aggressively probed deep into His rectum. Suddenly He did something He'd never done before. He passed gas. In my mouth. I was taken aback for a minute, but our agreement was my mouth was His, so I just inhaled and continued to rim Him. I was surprised how arousing the smell of His gas was. It was still His smell—that wonderful smell, just more intense. It inhaled deeply, felt my erection grow firmer, and kept licking and sucking away.

Sir swiftly turned around and apologized for His gas, which He explained was unintentional. I found myself telling Him I didn't mind and asking if He would do it again. He smiled. I continued to use my tongue to probe and lick Him and periodically He would fart. Each time I reveled in His smell and found myself getting harder and harder.

"I have to stop, boy," He said.

I asked Him what He meant and He said He hadn't had a bowel movement all weekend (this wasn't uncommon when Sir was traveling) and I'd gotten Him so wet and loosened up that He needed to go and go soon.

Sir and I had discussed His scat fantasies and of His desire to claim my mouth in this way. Thus far, neither of us had tried it. We were both scat virgins.

"I really have to go," He said.

"Go here, Sir." I smiled, pointing to my open mouth.

"Are you sure?" He asked.

I nodded.

"Are you sure?" I asked.

"Yes, but not here."

Sir led me to the shower stall just off the master bedroom and indicated that I should lie down face up. Our submissive dynamic aside, to me, we both seemed like two boys so excited to discover our new game, our new toy, that we could hardly spread out towels.

I admit I was nervous, but my excitement triumphed over my nerves. Plus, there was that smell. The smell that was responsible for this erection, the firmness of which I hadn't experienced since I was sixteen. I was ready.

Sir positioned Himself in a way that couldn't have been comfortable for Him—squatting close over my face while holding the heavy shower door posts with His hands.

"Are you okay, Sir?"

"More than." He looked back and smiled at me.

I lay my head back and continued to rim Him. I felt something shift in His body and held both halves of His butt to support Him. I could feel Him relaxing.

In retrospect, I didn't have to do much except lay there and be willing. I continued to lick as He directed and paused when He ordered. Finally the tip of my tongue came in contact with something very hard and pointy. It didn't have much of a taste, but I knew what was coming. Sir moaned and I watched His anus expand further and further. It was kind of magical to witness it. I experienced the smell most strongly now, and there were moments when I felt it was too strong for me, but I persevered. I watched it come out and kept my mouth wide open. It was dry, not wet and slippery at all. It didn't taste bad either. It smelled a bit like sulphur, but mostly of Him.

At the moment I felt it land in my mouth I began to convulse, spontaneously ejaculating, and Sir began to urinate all over my chest, stomach, and genitals. It was as if timing were perfect. When He was done, I didn't know what to do, so I just reached into my mouth and removed the still-firm piece and lay in on the shower floor next to me. Sir later laughed that He didn't quite know what to do either. He didn't expect me to eat it. I knew it would not be sexually exciting for Him to watch me eat it (and frankly I didn't want to), so it turned out the shower floor was the best choice. We did have quite a laugh over our mutual novice wondering, "Well, what the hell to do with this shit now?"

People might think it gross, like I did at one time, but it really felt like a communion—a boy being completely open to his Master and taking something sacred from his Master's body into his own mouth and body. I can't quite put the intensity of the connection into words, but can perhaps share a bit of what I've been taught about Native American spirituality: "Mouse, though low to the ground and observant of all miniscule details is often prey for Hawk and Eagle. In being consumed by Eagle or Hawk, Mouse becomes a part of these predatory birds and, in this joining, gets to soar high and see, not the details but the broad expanse of the earth below and the skies above."

In consuming something sacred from my Master, I had taken some of His uniquely personal power into me, making me a better boy, a stronger boy, and, ultimately, closer to the Man I loved.

The above account demonstrates both the power dynamic that is our current focus and the very intimate sharing and deep connection that many who engage in this kind of edge play discuss in online forums or in other interviews conducted for journalistic reporting. There is very, very little scientific research on this particular kind of sexual practice or interest. What little research there is tends to be individual cases based in psychiatric or forensic contexts with people who are suffering from a number of conditions or problems. Because of the lack of research and systematic studies, we are left with making conjectures and proposing tentative ideas about raunch play.

Geoff Mains discusses raunch play in *Urban Aboriginals*, and notes that the people he interviewed into watersports and scat mentioned (a) physical pleasure associated with elimination; (b) transgressing against social taboos around elimination; (c) the intimacy and sharing of something that is so private, socially, with another person; (d) humiliation and powerplay; and (e) ownership or territorial marking by the Dominant by having the submissive be the receiver of bodily fluids and excrement. Our own interviews and interactions with various parts of the BDSM subculture have also converged on these meanings and motivations by people who practice raunch play.

> In consuming something sacred from my Master, I had taken some of His uniquely personal power into me, making me a better boy, a stronger boy, and, ultimately, closer to the Man I loved.

The first two dynamics, pleasure and social taboos, have been key ideas used by psychologists when considering peoples' relations to urine and excrement. Early in the twentieth century, both psychoanalytic and learning theory/behaviorist approaches to human nature noted that the infant does not have an inborn or innate disgust or negative emotional reaction to the products of elimination. Anthropologists have also noted variation in how cultures emotionally react to urine and feces. All of these early approaches agreed that the social taboo is learned, imposed by the group, encultured within the toddler and young child as they develop in their first few years of life in human society. A negative squick factor as it relates to urine and feces, which appears to be intense and to develop early in childhood, is clearly a product of socialization.

Due to the intense socialization around it, scat play is greatly intertwined with both shame and power. In terms of scat play as an expression of power, there are many nuances and aspects that would demand more time and space than we have in this chapter—and it would be better to have that discussion once we have some facts, evidence, and detailed scientific exploration of the topic. In terms of an expression of power and the eroticization of power, however, we can clearly see that this kind of edge play can be used to enact a "dehumanization" frame on a particular BDSM scene, in terms of turning someone into a urinal or toilet. It can be used to signify more animalistic power expressions, such as marking territory. Using the products of elimination to mark someone as subordinate, submissive, or lower on the hierarchy also holds powerful symbolic value. The moment a submissive receives the Dominant's bodily excrement or urine is the moment there is an outward sign that the submissive will obey and allow the more powerful Dominant to do as He or She wishes.

In terms of our main exploration, this type of edge play has the same basic underlying psychological dynamic, albeit with a few particular, noteworthy differences, as impact play or 24/7 power-structured relationships. While the topic might inspire immediate and strong negative emotions in most people and, in fact, be controversial even among BDSM subcultures, it may not function much differently than other forms of erotic power exchange or kinky sexuality.

Age Play

Age play is the consensual manipulation of one's actual age by using fantasy, costuming, and props to create the illusion that one is either younger or older. As stated earlier, a person's experience or interest in playing a role that involves a marked difference in age, often as an expression of power differences, may occur for approximately a third of the people surveyed in some exploratory studies of BDSM activities and BDSM communities. Our culture organizes power along the dimension of age in some very pervasive ways, so it may not be surprising to find that people who eroticize power and power differentials might use the dimension of age as a way to organize their BDSM play.

Finding My girl (Sandra's Story)

Sandra wasn't a teacher, but she fantasized about being one.

In our work together we explored a series of fantasies that placed her in the seat of what she described aptly as "my power." Inside, she said, she "felt like a warrior," but outside, "I'm just some dumpy little secretary."

Sandra had some shame about being a lesbian and feeling like she didn't fit in either the Butch or the Femme camps. I would gently remind her that there were scores of lesbians in the world who didn't fit these stereotypes and that these traditional polarities of women-loving-women images were becoming less and less important. She used her playful humor both as a defense and as a means of connecting. She was smart and creative, and often thought in very grand mythological terms. I often imagined her as an ancient queen or a barmaid from the village of Bree, as she would describe herself with this type of archetypal imagery frequently.

"I could be the best queen at any Renaissance fair ever."

I heartily, and genuinely, agreed.

Sandra's difficulties began when she felt such a high degree of shame around her fantasies of power, particularly how they played out in relationship to age differentials, guidance, and discipline.

"Do you remember the covers of those lesbian pulp fiction novels from the late 1950s?" she asked me during one of our sessions.

"Yes."

"Do you remember the hot, Amazonian Dominatrix?"

"Which one?" I deadpanned.

Sandra shrieked, "Exactly! There were so many of them it was like a metaphor. No not a metaphor! An archetype. Is that right?"

"A modern one, yes."

"I mean, there were police officers, and oversexed mothers, and sadistic schoolteachers—and that's what I learned just from looking at the covers. So much for the stereotype that all we want to do is play softball and mow lawns!"

Sandra and I laughed together often and this was a good one.

"Tell me more," I said.

"I guess I developed a fantasy around what was written in those books, because I never looked inside—not until much later in life—and I was disappointed because what I found wasn't nearly as hot as what I'd been fantasizing and masturbating about since I was a teenager."

"What did you fantasize about?"

"Well, a whole bunch of different scenarios, but the one that stuck was the idea of me as a sexy school teacher. Maybe twenty-two years old, just out of college, but supremely feminine and hot."

"What do you look like?"

"Dark hair, pinned up into a tight French twist with sexy, almost Angelina Jolie–like makeup. Fierce black skirt suit, too short and cut too low, but conservative otherwise, except that it could never look conservative because my body is so hot it's bursting out."

"Tell me more about your body."

"Betty Page. That's all I can think of. Betty Page, but trying to look conservative and proper. Like a tight black suit with only a corset underneath. You see?"

"I'm envisioning it. Keep going."

"My breasts are big, pushed up and out. My waist is corseted tightly. Like a 36-25-36 would look if she was about five-nine."

"Talk like it's you," I gently corrected. For a woman with such a Domme streak, Sandra took redirection, especially from a man, incredibly well.

"Sorry. Okay—here goes! I am a smoking 36-25-36 Diva Domme and as tall as Uma Thurman! Long legs, seamed stocking with garters, supremely high heels. I'm getting really hot thinking of the power I have over the little high school freshman girls, all freshly showered and uniformed, who sit in my classroom filled with little desks—neatly organized in rows before me."

"That was powerfully described, Sandra. How did it feel?"

"I'm getting wet."

"What's it like to be that aroused here?"

"It's hot. I feel safe. You're gay. At least I think you're gay. Are you gay? I never asked! Ha! You're not going to take advantage of me. Are you?"

"Only by writing about you in my book."

"Oooooh good. I'll be a celebrity!"

"I'm changing the names."

Sandra mock-pouted. "Do you have to?"

"Yes," I said. "I have to."

"Oh, you're no fun."

"I know. It's tragic. Continue."

"You make me laugh!"

"Thanks. Laughter is good."

"I could never talk about this stuff if you didn't make me laugh, you know."

"Our joking around makes it more comfortable, right?"

"Totally."

"Well, I'm glad you're comfortable." I smiled. "So, what's next?"

"It's such a powerful role, you know?"

"The schoolteacher?"

"Any adult, really. I mean, when are we both at out most vulnerable and our most protected? Childhood, right? Times before the age of eighteen, when we're dependent upon teachers, parents, priests, nuns, crossing guards, gym teachers, coaches, guidance counselors, and camp leaders."

"Vulnerable and protected. I like how you phrased that—and the darker side of that would be?"

"Exactly what I am fantasizing about: being vulnerable and exploited. Well, exploited may be too strong of a word, but perhaps not."

"So, tell me your fantasy and maybe the words and concepts will become clearer through the narrative."

"So," Sandra settled into a corner of my sofa, tucked her legs beneath her, and brought her hands together with a light clap, as she often did when about to recount a story. "So those pulp fiction caricatures?"

"Yes."

"I find them so sexy and I feel like it's so wrong."

"How do you feel it's wrong?"

"Because, in my fantasy, I was to humiliate and punish one of the girls in front of the entire classroom."

I waited.

"Don't you think that's horrible?"

"Why do you think it's so horrible?"

"It's crossing a boundary."

"If you actually were a schoolteacher and were abusing a student, I would say you'd definitely be crossing a boundary, but you're not, and we're talking about a fantasy, so . . . no, I don't think there's anything horrible about transgressive fantasy."

Being shamed or staying in shame was something Sandra was used to and I didn't want to reinforce that by judging her fantasy, yet I knew it was appropriate to assess her risk for acting out her fantasy in reality.

"You're not planning on cruising any junior high school parking lots are you?"

"No!" she burst out laughing and mocked throwing my wicker tissue box at me.

My assessment went beyond this light interchange. After a few more questions, and given her high degree of impulse control, ethical understanding, and reality-monitoring, I was satisfied that Sandra represented no risk to anyone under the age of consent. Sandra didn't take offense at my questioning, either. She expressed that she knew I was just doing my job.

"Then we're good," I said. "So talk to me."

She went further than I would have thought.

She's the prettiest girl in the class. Bright-blonde hair, fair face, shy, and smart. Her name is April and she's so tender and vulnerable and beautiful, damn it! She's ethereal, untouchable. She has such power! She has power and so do I, but my power has authority painted all over it. I am the teacher and she's the student.

My power wins.

Corporal punishment is not only okay at my school; it's expected. Most of the girls have been forced to lay over my desk, lift their uniform skirts over their bottoms, and receive strokes with the cane I keep in the corner for such disciplinary sessions.

April was such a good girl. She never did anything to warrant even a scolding, but I often fantasized about finding an opportunity to get her over my desk and one day I got my wish. April sat between two girls named Ava and Maria who were more rebellious and prone to misbehavior. They'd been caned before for chewing gum, sassing me, and bullying the other girls at recess. This time, I watched as April passed a note to Ava.

"April!" I snapped.

"Yes, Ma'am."

"What is that?"

"A note, Ma'am. But Maria gave it to me to pass to Ava."

"Oh really." I folded my arms, watching her eyes begin to brim with tears. Even the suspicion that I didn't believe her was enough to make her teary.

I know full well that Maria and Ava are to blame, but I have the power to ignore that and finally have the opportunity to get April over my desk.

"April, stand up." April does as she's told and I marvel at how well-mannered and well-groomed she is, probably the most untouchable angel in the classroom. There is something intoxicating about knowing you have the power to drag the angel down from the heavens and roll her around in the dirt.

I drew out the two-and-a-half-foot rattan cane from behind my desk and April began to shake.

"Bend over the desk," I commanded, not needing to raise my voice. The room was so quiet it seemed to vibrate. The idea of April getting whipped? Unthinkable, and yet it was about to happen.

Instead of instructing her to lift her skirt, I reached down and lifted it ever so slowly, revealing the most perfectly round bottom I'd ever seen on a girl and the tightest little pink panties hugging her curves.

I am so thrilled right now, so high on the power I have over this girl I have spent a year lusting over. Knowing that she's really a very good girl, caught in a terrible misunderstanding only makes it more exciting.

I guide the cane through the air and it lands with a whisper of a crack against April's bottom. I hear her cry out and the class ooooohs and ahhhhhhhs.

Five more times I swish that cane against April's bottom and by now the surface of the desk is puddled with her tears. She's crying in earnest. No girl in my class has ever been caned more than six times and never on her bare bottom.

"April, I have never had to do this in all my years of teaching. Not only were you caught passing notes in class, but also you attempted to place the blame on two innocent students. For that, I will make an example of you that this class, and you, will never forget."

Slowly I pull down April's pink panties, and yank them over her ankle socks and patent-leather shoes. Pulling her skirt up higher, I leave her bent over the desk—her bare bottom on full display—while I walk to the bulletin board and pin her panties to it. By now the whole class is giggling and pointing at her. Her bottom bears six vivid, angry weals from the last six strokes.

"April, I am ashamed of your behavior as, no doubt, you parents will be when I inform them of your behavior today."

Now April's crying turns into begging,

"Please, Mistress, don't tell my mother and father. Plllleeeeeease!"

"We'll see," I barely whisper. "We'll see."

I deliver six more strokes of the cane against the fifteen-year-old's bare bottom and when I am through I let every girl in the classroom come up and take a look at the twelve raised welts that cover little April's once-perfect pink bottom. Some of the girls ask to see what it feels like and I allow them all to run their fingers over the ridges and marks covering April's behind while she remains bent over the desk still quietly weeping. I am reveling in April's humiliation and my complete power over her.

When I am satisfied, I send the girls back to their seats and send April to stand in the corner. She looks confused for a moment and silently points to her underwear, her eyes bloodshot and dazed.

"You'll remain after class today, April, and you and I will discuss wheth-
er you deserve to have your panties returned before you are sent home this
afternoon."

I spend the rest of the day continuing my lessons, looking over at April
quietly weeping in the corner and I wonder what she will be willing to do for
me after school to win back her little pink panties, and, if she fails to please
me, I wonder what her father and mother will do to her when they realize she
has come home without them. Do I even dare to imagine?

Sandra's fantasy was sexually charged because of its eroticizing power
through images of abuse, transgression, and discipline. I found it also an
imaginative way of viscerally expressing her anger at the lesbian community
for not allowing her to feel like she could fit into one of their strong butch/
femme extremes. She was caning a community, so to speak—very concretely
represented in the whipping of one of those extreme stereotypes (the vulnerable femme). She was also, in stature and power, channeling the archetypal
Virago.[10] Sandra agreed that she was likely working out some of her resent-
ments in this fantasy and perhaps even punishing the April in herself, expressing her disgust at her own femininity, the softness that kept her from
feeling a part of a larger butch community. I wonder if she would have, or
could have had, a similar catharsis had she enacted her powerful fantasy on a
very butch woman. From a perspective of personal responsibility, Sandra is
ultimately punishing herself for keeping herself apart from a community that
might very well accept her if she stopped viewing it only for its polarities and
continued to keep putting herself out there (which she doesn't). We recognize all of these potential interpretations while keeping in mind the reality
that age play is one of the strongest examples of erotic transgressions, and—
where lies the deepest shame and darkest secrets—is often where the most
extraordinary fantasies live.

Finding My girl (Lisa)

Traditionally, in heterosexual, gay, and lesbian communities, the use of the
words *boy* and *girl* often describe adult men and women who identify in
some way as submissive. An example would be "the boys of Leather" or "the
girls of Leather" club chapters in most major U.S. cities. Others use the title
boy or *girl* as part of their scene name. While others use it as a psychological
reminder to themselves and others that they are inhabiting a younger, more
vulnerable, and often submissive mind-set.

When Sandra spoke of finding her girl, she was referring to the archetypal
innocent youth represented in her fantasy by the sublime April. When Lisa
spoke about finding her girl, she was talking about the girl inside herself.
When I interviewed her, she'd been engaged in Teacher/student roleplays

with Sandra for over a year. Sandra, in our work, was less fixated on the butch/femme duality in the lesbian community and began to view herself and others with more compassion than when we started our work.

> I was lucky to find Sandra. My identity as a girl is "schoolgirl." It's how I dress and certainly how I see myself sexually. As a matter of fact, if you're observant enough, you can see an aspect or two of the typical schoolgirl's uniform in almost every outfit I wear. I look back on my childhood as a time of being powerless, but also a time of being taken care of by adults. There is an odd balance struck there between vulnerability and safety that is now inherently erotic to me.
>
> Sandra and I explored the fantasy above, and variants on it, many, many times. It's exciting to be able to give her what she wants and to see her living and breathing—*owning*—that power. I think it's a hard place for her to go, but she enjoys it and goes there more easily now. I love giving my power over to her.
>
> My power bores me. I am with it all day long. I'm barely thirty-five years old. I have two master's degrees and a law degree, and I hold a public office. Oh, and I write a nationally syndicated column. I am *tired* of being powerful. I never got in trouble at school. I was the smart, driven, charismatic kid. Now, I really do crave a strong warrior woman to pull me down off that glorified pedestal and remind me that inside me there's a little girl that needs to be controlled and roughed up a little. It's a welcome change.
>
> Plus, Sandra is hot, and she's an awesome bowler. Bet you didn't know that! She's got an average over 200. That's high! We love bowling too.
>
> —Lisa, thirty-four-year-old politician, academic, and schoolgirl (Portland, OR)

In bringing the story of Sandra and Lisa full circle, we emphasize the fact that it was the girl who helped the Teacher/Dominant let go of some of her rigidity around what it means to be a lesbian, particularly butch or femme. Lisa, though submissive and wholly the receiver of impact at the hands of her older and wiser (not to mention sadistic) schoolteacher, was actually lighting the path for Sandra toward a more integrated masculine and feminine sexuality and one in which she reportedly felt freer.

Voices of Age Play

> Sorry folks, Zac Efron, Brent Corrigan, and even Daniel Radcliffe were way hot before they were eighteen. That doesn't mean I'm gonna fuck them. But it also doesn't mean that I am going to deny the fact that boys can be beautiful, sexy even, long before they turn eighteen. Can't we say the same about Brad Pitt, Elijah Wood, and . . . do you want me to go on?
>
> I really think we do our young people a disservice by embracing a collective fantasy that their sexuality springs into being, fully formed, from the ether sometime around the age of 17 years and 364 days. It's not only inaccurate; it serves no one to deny that young people have erotic experiences and sexual feelings.

My seven-year-old nephew once pulled out his penis and said, "Why does it get like this sometimes?" He obviously had an erection and was clearly curious about it. I said, "Well, sometimes that happens to boys and men. Our penises get stiff, like yours is now. Sometimes it means we need to go pee and sometimes it just flexes on its own like a muscle." I didn't know what else to say! He was too young for any sexual information, yet I didn't want to shame him. "It's okay for you to talk about your penis, touch it, and even show it to me or your mom or dad when you have questions about it, like you just did. But, even though your penis is a part of your body and your body is a special and beautiful thing, Sean, it's also private, something very special that belongs just to you. So, except for when you're here at home, don't pull your penis out or point to it, or let anyone touch it—besides you—for right now. Okay?"

Sean agreed and I went on to explain the difference between "good touch" and "bad touch" to him. I had to think on my feet, but I genuinely believe there is a proper way to hold and engage a child's sexuality that recognizes that they are having experiences they may not understand without shaming them and without exploiting them. So we have to explain, within age-appropriate limits. It's our responsibility, as the adults they love and trust, to do what's best for the child in the moment.

—Michael, forty-one-year-old Gay Leatherman, kinkster, switch,
mental-health professional, and author (Washington, DC)

When discussing age play, it's important to make two points:

• Fantasy and reality are different.
• The realm of fantasy is not subject to ethics or law.

We rely on the awareness and impulse control of adult men and women to not confuse fantasy with reality.

It would be illegal to shoot your boss, as well as immoral in most religious and spiritual teachings. But how many of us have, at one time or another, fantasized about our employers falling victim to some wayward poison, as in the popular 1980 film *9 to 5*, or coming to a painfully splattered demise at the end of our own double-barrel shotgun?

Most of us would agree that sex with animals is inappropriate. Not because it is gross. We've already established that we have no interest in subjective judgments about gross. Sex with animals is not appropriate because you can't get an animal's consent, and nonconsensual sex is inappropriate. However, this does not stop us from enjoying the film *King Kong*, an essentially interspecies love story. In the film, particularly Peter Jackson's tender 2005 remake, the Great Ape and the equally great Naomi Watts fall in love—a wondrous, romantic, and emotional love. Follow this fact through logically and one can imagine that they perhaps enjoyed more intimate moments than looking at a sunset together. This is a love story of Titanic proportions. We cry at the end. It moves us.

But we do not go out and have sexual intercourse with apes or monkeys because we've seen the film.

> By reducing or increasing our ages in fantasy are we gaining or relinquishing more power than we feel we can handle? Or are we simply terrified of what people would think of us if they knew?

Similarly, there is no evidence to suggest that engaging in age play with your partner or fantasizing about playing with age dynamics will make you a pedophile. What is one of the greatest power differentials? Age. Younger people, youth, and children are often under the control, guidance, and sometimes at the mercy of their elders. Alternatively, sometimes a child has complete control of his or her parents in the moment of a tantrum. The inherent power imbalances in the childhood and teenage years mark it as fertile ground for some to begin fantasy explorations of power and power exchange.

My boyfriend, Danny, is twenty-four years old and looks about sixteen, except when he shaves off his pubic hair and the hair under his arms, which is the only body hair he has. Then he looks like he's about fourteen. I'm twenty-nine and look about twenty, tops. When I see he's shaved himself, it's my cue that he wants to begin one of our Big Brother/little brother roleplays. Our favorite is where I'm the older brother, home from college, masturbating to gay porn in my bedroom. Danny comes home early from junior high, still dressed in his eighth-grade track T-shirt and shorts, and decides to spy on me. He's always had a crush on his big brother. Well, he's not a very good spy and I catch him watching me and playing with himself and he gets a lesson he won't forget.

I slowly strip him completely. The last to go are his tight little track shorts, which I pull down slowly, elongating his humiliation from being stripped bare in my presence. Then I give him a good solid spanking, first with my hand, and then with my belt. Only when he's apologized and is begging for mercy do I stop. I gather him up into my arms and hold him tightly, stroking his bottom and telling him how proud I am of him, how much I love him, and how happy I am that he's my little brother. Once he's comfortable and has come down from the whipping, I gently, but firmly, initiate him into the world of man-on-man sex. He plays at resisting me, but I always find creative ways to wear him down until he finally submits to every desire I have. The scenes usually culminate in me taking his virginity. It's hot for him and hot for me. We'll probably be together forever because, with our imaginations, things won't get boring.

Also, I love him very much.

—Nick, twenty-nine-year-old boyfriend, tech systems analyst, Dom, and Big Brother to Danny (Oakland, CA)

Age play is one of the most forbidden topics in sexual roleplay and kink. Is it because we are ashamed of it? Disgusted by it? Turned on by it? Do we fear that exploring those waters will make us a pedophile or sex offender? By reducing or increasing our ages in fantasy are we gaining or relinquishing more power than we feel we can handle? Or are we simply terrified of what people would think of us if they knew?

If you're ever aroused watching the budding boyish masculinity of River Phoenix in *Stand By Me* or by the nubile, street-smart Jodie Foster in *Taxi Driver*, that doesn't make you ipso facto a pedophile.[11] In fact, it may mean that you simply have great taste in physical beauty or in acting talent. Or both.

If we sound offhand about a serious topic, it's because we write from a confusing cultural binary. Our society is alternately in states of sexual saturation and sexual denial. We face the same conundrum with age play and age-related discussions of sex, eroticism, and beauty. How can we deny or claim to not see the Eros in youthful beauty when we live in a culture and society that literally deifies it? We cannot worship it on one hand, and on the other hand pretend that it's not really there to begin with. It's illogical and crazy-making.

In a culture where we seek beauty and youth at all costs, exemplified by the pursuit of extensive plastic surgery or the popularity of baby-doll and beach-boy haute couture, the shadow side of that obsession is wanting to tear down that beautiful, youthful innocent ideal. We revere it, we envy it, and we also despise it. Nature seems to keep making younger and younger people, reminding us all of our own eventual decay and death. Is it difficult to imagine that we worship and covet on one hand and envy and wish to tear down on the other?

So we worship youth and beauty in the sublime forms of Lindsay Lohan today or Robert Downey Jr. in the mid-1990s and attempt to emulate their youthful looks, and then we gawk with fascination and pleasure when they go down in the flames of substance abuse and emotional turmoil. We don't want to see youthful beauty thrive, though we oddly revere and covet it. Perhaps we wish to destroy what we can't have any longer, especially when it's an object we also secretly desire.

> Our society is alternately in states of sexual saturation and sexual denial.

Perhaps age play creates a space where some of these feelings and desires can be realized and enjoyed where no one under the age of consent is actually at risk. This can be a co-created space, like Nick and Sean have, where adults can be at once adults and also children, thus underscoring the word *play*. Sexual play can be playful. It's allowed. If we allow it.

THE CONNECTING THREAD

At the beginning of the chapter, we set out to demonstrate that a major motivational factor in BDSM sexualities, and one that is expressed in the events, rituals, and practices of BDSM communities, is the attraction to power as an aphrodisiac. Power differences and power exchanges are a great source of erotic electricity for people practicing kinkier forms of sex. Even though the surface expression of people's sexualities can be different, even uniquely different when you pay attention at a fine-grained level of detail, there is a connecting thread that is core to understanding BDSM sexualities and communities: the eroticization of power.

In following that thread through the five different expressions we explored, a number of key ideas emerged. It is possible that the eroticization of power is similar to sexual orientation, that some people are more oriented to erotic power exchange than other people. If so, the development and the nature/nurture sources of an erotic orientation to power are probably similar to the development and nature/nurture aspects of sexual orientation. The concept of "coming out" around a stigmatized sexuality is also probably the same. There is a richness to this idea, and calls for further study. In addition, power exchange as a way of intimately relating to another poses a challenge and a question to the American cultural emphasis on individuality and independence as the most important hallmarks of a healthy human being. Some of these assumptions underlie Western ideas of mental health and well-being, and the 24/7 power-structured relationship challenges those Western ideals.

Exhibitionism and voyeurism are drenched in power differences, yet the particular thread of eroticizing power highlights that there is a strong dialectic about power differences: the same person is both powerful and powerless when that person is an object of viewing. There is power in being able to inspire erotic desire in the voyeur; there is powerlessness in being the object of inspection or viewing. This is a key aspect about power and it becomes an erotic resource used by kinky people. BDSM subcultures have developed and explored this dialectic in a sophisticated manner. BDSM communities acknowledge that the submissive has a notable degree of power in BDSM interactions and relationships.

Impact play raises serious questions about the nature of violence and aggression and, we believe, highlights that physical force is not the same as violence or aggression, and that any act of violence needs to be understood in light of the involved people's intentions and understandings. This idea lies close to the overarching point of view we take in this book: the surface appearance of an action or behavior is an unreliable indicator of the psychological meaning and impact. Society readily recognizes this in many areas of life, and the same approach should be applied to understanding BDSM.

Our investigation into two areas of edge play and their relation to power demonstrated that breaking or transgressing strong social taboos brings an erotic thrill and an intense sense of vulnerability. That vulnerability allows for an expression of erotic power exchange, and the breaking of a social taboo that doesn't feel consistent with one's experience or worldview can lead to a great sense of empowerment. Edge play, because it goes beyond the hegemonic boundaries of mainstream society, also creates a space of deep bonding between participants—we are out here on the edge and that is a scary and thrilling place. It's an intense realm.

Edge play teaches us that erotic power gets its juice from being an outsider, from being on the edges of what is considered safe and proper. This edge is dangerous territory, a place in the human psyche where the Shadow dwells. In such territory, exploration becomes a boon, if the knowledge from the exploration is brought back to the home space.

Our sexual outsiders walk an edge, and doing so gives them a power that is wild, uncivilized, and untamed and, like fire, it can be a source of harm as well as good. The tipping point between beneficial gains or harmful consequences comes down to acceptance and understanding, fostered in connection to a thriving community. Even if we don't fully understand, or we have strong squick reactions to a variety of kinky behaviors, we can understand that eroticizing power is a driving motivation for many sexual outsiders.

Chapter Seven

Getting Assistance

I loved my Jungian psychotherapist. My dreams often reflect my state of mind and that sort of exploration in therapy was helpful. I finally had to leave though because she had no idea about queer sexuality or BDSM. She wasn't judgmental or crass about it; she just didn't know what I was talking about. After a while, it felt like I was spending our sessions educating her and that wasn't what I needed to be doing to take care of myself.

—Jessie, twenty-seven-year-old queer-identified kinky woman (Richmond, VA)

No matter how well one comes to understand what BDSM is, to navigate the waters as a curious novice, to engage in a coming-out process, to meet one's Shadow and learn to embrace it, or to deal with the reality of things sometimes going awry, there are still often unanswered questions and a need for additional guidance and support. Like the rest of the general population, people practicing BDSM may find themselves in a time or situation when they need to consult with a medical, therapeutic, or legal professional. Even with supportive partners, a loving spouse, strong mentors, or open-minded family members, sometimes a person needs the professional perspective of an individual not involved in their daily lives and relationships, someone who can be more objective, someone who can lend their expertise.

As psychological and therapeutic professionals, we are going to focus on some of the ways members of BDSM communities can seek help from members of our profession in a healthy, affirming manner. Some of the resources we present can be used to find professionals in a number of fields. Since neither of us works with clients who are mandated by courts or governmental agencies to enter therapy, our discussion of the therapeutic process is based on our experiences with clients who enter therapy voluntarily. These are individuals who seek therapy as a resource for personal growth, whether the goals of that growth include recovering from trauma; addressing sexual needs, desires, or conflicts; exploring relationship dynamics; addressing personality dynamics; managing moods; or finding a more authentic way to be themselves. This kind of therapeutic work is accomplished through inquiry and analysis into a patient's personal values and motivations that guide them toward their goals.

Be it psychotherapy, counseling, sex therapy, bodywork, or the various forms of psychoanalysis, therapy is a reciprocal and symbiotic relationship. No client-therapist relationship is exactly like another. Therapists and patients are co-creators of an experience that is germane to them. As a patient or client, it takes a tremendous amount of courage and faith to make that initial phone call, to enter the office of a complete stranger with the expectation that you will begin to divulge the most intimate details of your life. Therapists have tremendous power and an equally tremendous responsibility not to interject their own moral and political philosophies into treatment and, perhaps most importantly, to be discerning and conservative when assigning clinical diagnoses. Diagnostic labels often follow a client throughout his or her life and can impact their access to affordable medical care in the future.

It is equally incumbent upon the patient to be a savvy consumer when selecting a therapist. When discussing issues of sexuality, especially forms of sexuality such as BDSM that are almost always viewed as outside the norm, it is crucial that the prospective patient select a therapist with a broad sexual mind, one that is well educated and informed (both psychosexually and culturally) about the spectrum of human sexuality and, above all, is not intimidated or reluctant to talk about sexuality in a candid manner. In selecting a therapist, an educated consumer will be a satisfied consumer.

Often this means asking questions. A therapist who is uncomfortable or unwilling to answer your questions about his or her familiarity with topics that are significant to you is probably not going to be the best choice. Perhaps one of the focuses of your work is to understand the nature of your own sexual desires, and you're looking for a therapist who can help you get from where you are sexually to where you want to be. You may have fantasies you wish to understand, or act out. Or understand and not act out. Perhaps you're struggling with how to communicate newly discovered desires with your partner or partners, or maybe you're looking for some validation that your desires and fantasies are not inherently unhealthy, immoral, or wrong.

Understanding what you want out of therapy, like understanding what you want out of any relationship, will help you find the right person, a steadfast companion, to support you in reaching whatever goals you have set for yourself, one who can help you travel the roads of your own personal growth.

BDSM EDUCATION: AN ISSUE OF CULTURAL COMPETENCY

Within the professional fields that provide counseling, therapy, or mental-health services, there is an increasing concern around multicultural sensitivity. There is a great need for adequate training to increase the competency of mental-health professionals regarding issues of human diversity. Globalization is leading to an increased diversity in the backgrounds, cultures, and perspectives of people seeking therapy. Given the ethical foundation that helps guide the provision of mental-health services, a therapist needs to be able to address the needs of people who are different from him or her, or have the knowledge and ability to refer them to a more appropriate practitioner. In response to this need for multicultural sensitivity, many professional organizations, state government licensing boards, and educational programs have all begun to emphasize the need for cultural diversity in the practice of therapy.

While these changes are helpful, the same emphasis around sexuality has not occurred. In many educational and training programs for future therapists, entire semester-long classes on multicultural diversity are expected. These classes amount to approximately forty-five hours of class time. But in many of these same programs, required human sexuality courses amount to only about six to twelve hours.

The intersection of cultural diversity and sexuality is not really addressed by most graduate programs, or the state board requirements overseeing the licensing of therapists and counselors, or professional organizations, except in a very abbreviated way. BDSM sexuality, as practiced by many people, is part of a subculture. It should, logically, be approached as an issue of cultural diversity, alongside gay, lesbian, bisexual, and transgender issues, and cultural issues surrounding marriage, family, and other intimate relationships. In our experience, it takes more than twelve hours to learn about BDSM sexuality in a manner that would prepare a counselor or therapist to provide competent, sensitive, and effective therapy.

In the Kink/BDSM communities, there is a great dearth of culturally competent counselors and therapists. By our estimation, there are approximately five hundred kink-friendly or kink-identified clinicians in the United States and Canada, and there are approximately five million people who are kink-identified or even just kinky on a semi-regular basis. That would be about one well-trained therapist for every ten thousand kinky people, a staggering ratio that leaves many of our sexual outsiders still very much outside.

In 2008, the National Coalition for Sexual Freedom[1] authored a report that collected incidents, stories, and feedback from people in the BDSM communities about their experience of stigma and prejudice. The survey had 3,058 respondents, and 37.5 percent of those had experienced some sort of discrimination, harassment, or prejudice. Approximately one out of nine

BDSM community members had experienced prejudice or discrimination from a professional service provider. One hundred thirty-six people, specifically, had horrible experiences with therapists and counselors. These are the people we call "therapy refugees." In their report, the NCSF also collected sixty-three comments from kink-identified clients interacting with therapists and counselors who were culturally incompetent. Here are some of their quotes:

"The therapist refused to continue to see me until I acknowledged that I was being 'abused.'"

"I was told that my depression was due to my participation in BDSM activities and lifestyle practices. She said that if I stopped the 'negative' behaviors I would feel better. Instead I stopped seeing her and continued to full recovery. I am also so proud of my involvement that I did a speech in my women's studies class about how submission is not a sign of a weak woman, and I worked hard to dispel a lot of the myths attributed to living in BDSM. I am also writing a book about my life and how this has helped me in my journey toward self-discovery and self-worth."

"I was made to feel like I am not normal and a social deviant. I felt uncomfortable and felt I could not freely be myself or talk openly about issues concerning myself to my psychologist. I spent more than half of one of my sessions trying to defend myself and my position in the BDSM community."

"I was told by several mental health professionals that my desires to inflict pain on another, albeit willing, participant was deviant and I needed to deal with my anger and bigotry issues."

"After finding out about my interest in BDSM, my psychiatrist stated that I 'cannot be ruled out as a danger to myself or others due to my interest in BDSM.'"

"I told a psychologist once about my involvement with BDSM and he told me that he thought it was unsafe and not a wise choice. I told him that it was indeed safe, and he seemed to just roll his eyes and move on."

"I was in therapy for six months and didn't feel safe enough to tell my therapist about my SM orientation."

"I was told by a licensed psychologist that I was a sick individual, and that if I did not get help immediately, and change the way I lived, that I would never have a productive life, and that I would never find any happiness. By fitting into the 'norm,' I would be a more socially 'productive' person, and I would be able to live a 'normal' life."

"After an off-hand comment made by the therapist about 'those sick people who beat each other,' I was put into a position of being unable to talk about any connections I had to BDSM. I also felt that it was unsafe to discuss that I was raped by a partner (which was something I needed to talk about) because we had been involved in a Dom/sub relationship."

"A therapist I saw in San Francisco from 1992 to 1998 had a very strong reaction to my involvement in BDSM. This was surprising because she had been so understanding and supportive of my choice to do sex work. In early 1998 I began getting more involved in BDSM and shared this with my therapist. We had arguments about it. She told me it was 'disgusting' and that I was 'killing live cells'—as if I wasn't doing this every time I went out in the sun or brushed my teeth. Her attitude toward me changed dramatically. She had been very helpful as a therapist until I came out to her about BDSM. I ended the therapy shortly afterward."

THE BDSM AND THERAPY PROJECT

In 2007, CARAS (Community Academic Consortium for Research on Alternative Sexualities) developed the BDSM and Therapy Project to increase the knowledge and skills of therapists when serving people within BDSM communities and to educate community members about high-quality therapy and how to interact with mental-healthcare providers around sexual and erotic material.

"I was in therapy for six months and didn't feel safe enough to tell my therapist about my SM orientation."

The project documents best practices for therapy, from the dual points of view of members of the Kink community and therapists with extensive experience with BDSM sexualities. The project produced a film that explores common barriers to high-quality therapy and mental-health services as experienced by men and women within BDSM communities and also serves as a training resource for counselors and therapists, demonstrating aspects of culturally competent care for working with clients who express BDSM sexuality.

The following vignettes are taken from the BDSM and Therapy Project film.

This scene takes place after an initial client/therapist consultation during which a life history and a psychosocial evaluation of the client has been performed by the treating therapist.

DR. ROBBINS: Come in, Mr. Ellis. It's nice to see you again.

MR. ELLIS: Thank you, Dr. Robbins. I gotta say, I was a bit anxious during that whole life history thing we did last week.

DR. ROBBINS: It's natural to feel a bit nervous at first. I hope you're feeling more comfortable today.

MR. ELLIS: Uh, kinda. (pause) Nah, I'm still kinda anxious.

DR. ROBBINS: Well, I appreciate your honesty. Sit down, please, and let's see what we can do for you today.

DR. ROBBINS: Now, let's take look at the concerns that came out of our last session, shall we? You expressed a difficulty communicating with your partner about your needs. You talked about a decrease in sexual arousal compared to what you were feeling, and enjoyed feeling, on a regular basis earlier in your relationship.

MR. ELLIS: That about sums it up.

DR. ROBBINS: So, let's begin with communication. What is it that you are having trouble communicating about?

MR. ELLIS: Mostly sex.

DR. ROBBINS: (good-naturedly) So we've moved right on to number two now, have we?

MR. ELLIS: Well, no. (becoming frustrated) Damn. It's all kinda mixed up in there all together!

DR. ROBBINS: Okay, well let's take a step back and look at this. (pause) What is it about sex that is difficult to communicate about?

MR. ELLIS: Well, that's complicated.

DR. ROBBINS: How is it complicated, Mr. Ellis?

MR. ELLIS: (tentatively questioning) You're a psychotherapist and a sex therapist, right?

DR. ROBBINS: Yes, I am. We discussed my qualifications at our first meeting. Do you have a concern you'd like to express?

MR. ELLIS: Well, gosh, no. It's just that . . . you've . . . heard, I guess . . . a lot of stuff in here before, huh?

DR. ROBBINS: Yes, Mr. Ellis, I have heard quite a bit.

(Long pause during which the therapist remains completely focused on the patient.)

MR. ELLIS: It's not a big problem.

DR. ROBBINS: Alright. But it was big enough to bring you here, correct?

MR. ELLIS: Yeah, you nailed that one, Doc. (uncomfortable laughter) See, when my wife and I started playing. . . .

DR. ROBBINS: Playing?

MR. ELLIS: Yeah. Like . . . having sex.

DR. ROBBINS: Oh. (pause) Continue.

MR. ELLIS: Well when we started playing, and we always play together, no other partners or anything like that. . . .

DR. ROBBINS: You're monogamous.

MR. ELLIS: Yeah, even at play parties.

DR. ROBBINS: (Quizzical look)

MR. ELLIS: So when we started playing, I wasn't in as good a shape as I am now. I've been working out a lot, cutting my muscles up, getting my weight down. . . .

DR. ROBBINS: That sounds wonderful for you.

MR. ELLIS: Well, yeah . . . in some ways. Before the exercise results started showing, my wife used to flog me real gentle, you know a nice warm build-up, some pain, but good pain, you know? But since my body's gotten all buff, she gets really excited and likes to lay that flogger on so hard, so fast. She says all this heavy stuff like, "I am gonna cut that back up, boy, and throw salt on it and leave you hanging there for all the sailors to see come morning!"

DR. ROBBINS: I don't understand the sailor reference.

MR. ELLIS: Oh . . . that's just a fantasy we play out. She's, like, the mean ship's captain and I'm the cabin boy who keeps screwing up, so she has to punish me.

DR. ROBBINS: So you let your wife beat you?

MR. ELLIS: No, she doesn't beat me; she flogs me with a leather flogger when we play out our scenes together.

DR. ROBBINS: And this is okay with you? I mean, to have your wife be abusive and sadistic to you?

MR. ELLIS: No, it's not like that. It's part of how we play, have sex.

DR. ROBBINS: And you . . . like it when your wife flags you?

MR. ELLIS: Flogs me.

DR. ROBBINS: (flustered) Yes, flogs you. You like it?

MR. ELLIS: Yeah, I like it a lot! Is there something wrong with that?

DR. ROBBINS: Well, it's uncommon, in my experience. But, continue.

MR. ELLIS: So, I need to find a way to communicate to her that I need her to slow down and give me more warm up, but I don't want to ruin her Dominant headspace and I don't want to ruin my submissive headspace by making a request of her, you know?

DR. ROBBINS: So, you are submissive to your wife and she is Dominant over you?

MR. ELLIS: Not all the time, but when we play, yes.

DR. ROBBINS: And you like this?

MR. ELLIS: I'm sorry, Doctor, but why are you asking that question again? You just asked it a few seconds ago.

DR. ROBBINS: Mr. Ellis, in order for this to work, I need you to let me ask the questions for now.

MR. ELLIS: Okay, sorry.

DR. ROBBINS: So there is no opportunity for you to just say to her, "Honey, can you flog me a little lighter?"

MR. ELLIS: I would never call her "honey" in a scene.

DR. ROBBINS: Why not?

MR. ELLIS: It would be disrespectful. I call her Ma'am or Captain.

DR. ROBBINS: So, does your wife always have difficulty accepting loving terms, such as *honey* from you?

MR. ELLIS: No! Just when we're in the scene. I can't ask her then. It might wreck the scene for her, and me.

DR. ROBBINS: So the real problem is communication.

MR. ELLIS: Well, yeah, I guess.

DR. ROBBINS: So, how do you communicate and come to decisions when you are, say, buying groceries for the family?

MR. ELLIS: We just talk about it right then and there and decide mutually.

DR. ROBBINS: Well, it sounds like you have your solution right there.

MR. ELLIS: No, that way wouldn't work. I am trying to explain to you, that it's hard to talk about it right then and there. I need advice on how to bring it up, and when.

DR. ROBBINS: Mr. Ellis, you are beginning to get defensive. Take a couple of deep breaths and tell me what you are feeling.

MR. ELLIS: I am feeling that you don't get it.

DR. ROBBINS: Try taking the breaths.

(Mr. Ellis takes three deep breaths.)

MR. ELLIS: I am feeling like we're not getting to the issue. I just want to know how to communicate with my wife sexually, about this, but not ruin her Dom space or my sub space.

DR. ROBBINS: Okay, so let's talk about what happens right before you begin these . . . flogging scenes.

MR. ELLIS: Well she'll tie my hands up over my head to the bedpost or canopy. . . . We pretend it's a ship—

DR. ROBBINS: Wait . . . I apologize for interrupting you, but you mentioned a bedpost? I thought you said you did this kind of sex play at parties?

MR. ELLIS: Well yeah, but a lot of times we do it at home, you know, as a warm up to sex, or just as the sex itself, you know?

(Dr. Robbins stops paying attention and begins rifling through his notes.)

MR. ELLIS: So, before I know it, I am tied all up and the chance to actually talk about it has passed and—

DR. ROBBINS: Mr. Ellis, I need to stop you for a moment. You have . . . two children . . . a daughter named Claire, age seven, and a son named Bobby who is twelve, correct?

MR. ELLIS: Uh . . . yeah. But, what's that got to do with this?

DR. ROBBINS: Mr. Ellis, you're being defensive again. I need you to relax.

MR. ELLIS: But you keep changing the subject. I want to talk about—

DR. ROBBINS: Has it ever occurred to you or to your wife the effects your lifestyle might have on your children?

MR. ELLIS: What are you talking about?

DR. ROBBINS: Well, for example, what if they heard their mother yelling profanities—

MR. ELLIS: We don't swear during our scenes—

DR. ROBBINS: Or heard their father screaming—

MR. ELLIS: She usually gags me, which is why I can't ask her to go slower—

DR. ROBBINS: Or found whips and chains lying about—

MR. ELLIS: Okay . . . hey!

DR. ROBBINS: Mr. Ellis, I must ask that you not interrupt me.

MR. ELLIS: With all due respect, Doctor, you interrupted me.

DR. ROBBINS: I am not going to engage in a power struggle with you.

MR. ELLIS: We don't do scenes when the kids are home. We don't even use chains! Any toys we have are locked in a chest in our closet—

DR. ROBBINS: Whips are not toys, Mr. Ellis.

MR. ELLIS: There! See! You just did it again.

DR. ROBBINS: Well, I am sorry you *feel* interrupted, but I am concerned about the effects this whole thing could be having on your children.

MR. ELLIS: Look, my wife and I are very discreet. I already told you we don't play when the kids are home. Not only that, but *all* adults have sex—

DR. ROBBINS: Well, not all. . . .

MR. ELLIS: *Most* adults have sex and part of being an adult is knowing how to use discretion. That's why doors and closets have locks.

(The awkward pause here serves as a standoff of sorts.)

MR. ELLIS: You're not going to be able to help me have this conversation with my wife, are you?

DR. ROBBINS: I am perfectly able to help you have this conversation with your wife, but I think it's more important that we (a) discuss how this may or may not be affecting your children and (b) find some of the underlying reasons why you are unable to accept love without pain.

MR. ELLIS: I *can* accept love without . . . look, this is useless. You are *so* not dealing with the issues I have.

DR. ROBBINS: On the contrary, Mr. Ellis, it is you who is so not dealing with the issues you have.

MR. ELLIS: I don't think I want to work with you.

DR. ROBBINS: I am sorry you feel that way.

MR. ELLIS: It's nothing personal. It's just that, well, you don't get it.

DR. ROBBINS: Oh, I do get it, believe me. I just don't get it in the way you want me to.

MR. ELLIS: (slightly confused, upset) So, um, can you refer me to someone else who might understand this . . . I mean understand my situation a little bit . . . uh, better?

DR. ROBBINS: I am sorry to disappoint you, Mr. Ellis, but any decent therapist is probably going to have the exact same reaction I just did.

MR. ELLIS: You mean you're not going to give me a referral?

DR. ROBBINS: I simply don't know anyone who would be able to tell you anything more than what I have.

MR. ELLIS: (rising to leave) There's no, like, referral guide?

DR. ROBBINS: Not that I am aware of. May I suggest looking on the Internet or in one of the gay papers.

MR. ELLIS: But we're not gay!

DR. ROBBINS: Yes, but sometime those papers have professional advertisements that deal with more . . . alternative situations. Now, I really must tell you, our time is up.

(Therapist dismissively begins to go through the papers in his lap.)

(Patient just stands there.)

DR. ROBBINS: Good *day*, Mr. Ellis.

(Patient turns and exits.)

How might things have been different for Frank Ellis had he known to seek out a therapist who was both comfortable with the subject of sexuality and was also kink aware? Let's take a look.

DR. ROBBINS: Come in, Mr. Ellis. It's nice to see you again.

MR. ELLIS: Thank you, Dr. Robbins. I gotta say, I was a bit anxious during that whole life history thing we did last week.

DR. ROBBINS: It's natural to feel a bit nervous at first. I hope you're feeling more comfortable today.

MR. ELLIS: Uh, kinda. (pause) Nah, I'm still kinda anxious.

DR. ROBBINS: (smiling) Well, I appreciate your honesty. Sit down, please, and let's see what we can do for you today. Let's take a look at some of the issues that came out of our last session, alright? You expressed a difficulty communicating with your partner about your needs. You talked about a decrease in sexual arousal compared to what you were feeling, and enjoyed feeling, on a regular basis earlier in your relationship.

MR. ELLIS: That about sums it up.

DR. ROBBINS: So, why don't we begin with looking at some of the specific things that are difficult for you to communicate about with your partner.

MR. ELLIS: Okay. We communicate real well, almost all of the time. We have a great relationship and a great love life . . . it's just that . . . sometimes . . . oh, it's all so complicated!

DR. ROBBINS: Has it always been complicated?

MR. ELLIS: No.

DR. ROBBINS: Has something changed lately to make it more complicated?

(Silence.)

DR. ROBBINS: Mr. Ellis, you seem a little frightened. Is this hard for you to talk about today?

MR. ELLIS: Yes. No. I mean . . . I guess I am feeling a little . . .

(Pause.)

DR. ROBBINS: Inhibited? Shy?

MR. ELLIS: Yes, I am feeling shy, and a little embarrassed. I've never talked to a therapist about sex before. I only talk about sex with my wife and a few good friends. My parents didn't talk about sex at all. It was sort of a taboo subject.

DR. ROBBINS: That's unfortunate. Sex is a great thing, and obviously something you and your wife have enjoyed a lot. We live in a society that discourages us from talking about sex openly and that can result in feelings of shame or embarrassment. It's fine to acknowledge those feelings and move through them. I understand what you're feeling.

MR. ELLIS: You do?

DR. ROBBINS: Of course. It's difficult for many of us to talk about the intimate details of our sex lives with strangers, and that's what I still am to you, right? A stranger.

MR. ELLIS: I'm sorry but, yeah, it still feels like you're a stranger.

DR. ROBBINS: That's fine. The more we work together, the more you'll learn to trust in our relationship, the safety and confidentiality in this room, and you'll be able to open up more.

MR. ELLIS: But I want to fix this problem now, not three months from now.

DR. ROBBINS: Well, there's one way to attempt that.

MR. ELLIS: How?

DR. ROBBINS: Trust me now, even though you have feelings of shyness and reservation. Talk to me now just as though you were talking to a friend.

MR. ELLIS: Okay. I'll try.

DR. ROBBINS: Good. I appreciate your taking this risk with me, Mr. Ellis.

MR. ELLIS: Would it be okay if I asked you to call me Frank?

DR. ROBBINS: Yes, it's okay to ask for that, and I'll be happy to call you Frank.

MR. ELLIS: Ummm . . .

(Short pause.)

DR. ROBBINS: Would it be easier if I let you call me Michael instead of Dr. Robbins?

MR. ELLIS: (relieved) Yes, it really would. Thanks, Michael.

DR. ROBBINS: You're very welcome. Okay, Frank, let's look at this together. What's changed?

MR. ELLIS: Well when my wife and I started playing together, I wasn't in as good a shape as I am now. I've been working out a lot, cutting my muscles up, getting my weight down. . . .

DR. ROBBINS: Congratulations. That sounds great for you.

MR. ELLIS: Well, yeah . . . in some ways. Before the exercise results started showing, my wife used to flog me real gentle, you know a nice warm build up, some pain, but good pain, you know. But since my body's gotten all buff, she gets really excited and likes to lay that flogger on so hard, so fast! She says all this heavy stuff like, "I am gonna cut that back up, boy, and throw salt on it and leave you hanging there for all the sailors to see come morning!"

DR. ROBBINS: So, I think it's safe to say that you and your wife engage in some BDSM and powerplay in your sex lives?

MR. ELLIS: Oh, yes. A lot, actually.

DR. ROBBINS: Does she hit you against your will, or without your consent?

MR. ELLIS: No, never.

DR. ROBBINS: Do you feel comfortable being submissive to her sexually?

MR. ELLIS: Oh yeah, sure. I love it. I've loved it ever since my first girl-friend in college tied my hands up with one of her hair scrunchies and took me right there on the floor of my dorm room.

DR. ROBBINS: That sounds like it was an exciting sexual breakthrough for you.

MR. ELLIS: It was. It opened my eyes to this whole world of pleasure and pain.

DR. ROBBINS: But now, it sounds like the changes in your body have gotten your wife more erotically charged lately and her excitement is influencing the intensity of her floggings.

MR. ELLIS: Yes, and sometimes it hurts, I mean . . . it's supposed to hurt. . . . Oh, this is so hard to explain. . . .

DR. ROBBINS: Frank, there is a difference between the good kind of pain that gets you excited and sets your mind spinning into an erotic realm and the unpleasant pain that takes you out of a scene.

DR. ROBBINS: Yeah, that's it.

DR. ROBBINS: So, is your wife supportive of you when you ask her for more warm-up time, or perhaps a lighter-weight flogger?

MR. ELLIS: No.

DR. ROBBINS: Frank, I've got to be honest. It surprises me that she wouldn't be supportive of you, especially when you tell me that you're so close and that communication has always been healthy and open up 'til now.

MR. ELLIS: Oh, no. She's not supportive because I haven't been able to talk to her about it yet.

DR. ROBBINS: I see. So what's holding you back, Frank?

MR. ELLIS: I can't figure out how to tell her that I need her to slow down and give me more warm up, because I don't want to ruin her Dominant headspace and I don't want to ruin my submissive headspace by making a request of her, you know?

DR. ROBBINS: I can understand that. Do you and your wife have a safeword for when things get too intense?

MR. ELLIS: Yes. Arugula.

DR. ROBBINS: Well, that's one I haven't heard yet.

MR. ELLIS: We like to cook.

DR. ROBBINS: That's great. Is there something that's keeping you from using the safeword with her?

MR. ELLIS: Well, it's kind of an ego thing, I guess. I really get off on being able to take whatever she dishes out during a scene. I could break it with a safeword and I know she'd understand, but it would totally ruin it for me sexually, and I'd feel like such a wimp.

DR. ROBBINS: Well, I think it's important that you recognize that having some sensation limits doesn't make you a wimp, Frank. But I do understand how a submissive would want to do their best to endure what a Dominant delivers. How do you feel when a scene is over and you've taken everything your wife has given you?

MR. ELLIS: I'm pumped! I feel so proud, excited, and honorable. It's so hot! And then afterward, when all those endorphins are released, we can lay in bed and hold each other. Sometimes, she'll massage my back and we'll make love; I don't want to fuck all that up. . . . Is it okay to say *fuck*?

DR. ROBBINS: Would you say *fuck* if you were talking to a friend?

MR. ELLIS: Uh, yeah.

MR. ELLIS: Then it's okay to say *fuck* here. Frank, I am here to help you figure this out and have you be comfortable. Don't concern yourself with my being comfortable. I'm perfectly at ease with our conversation.

MR. ELLIS: Thanks. 'Cause this is hard to talk about.

DR. ROBBINS: I know. So, Frank, what I'm hearing is that your wife is having a very erotically charged response to the changes in your body and that excitement is bringing her into a play space that is a little rougher than what you're used to without some significant warm-up.

MR. ELLIS: Yes.

DR. ROBBINS: And, because a piece of your submission hinges on pleasing her, you're choosing not to break the scene with a safeword so you can feel proud and fulfilled.

MR. ELLIS: Yes.

DR. ROBBINS: So, I think the best way to handle this would be to talk with her about your limits and need for an elongated warm-up, outside the context of the scene, either right before you decide to play, or right after when you're cuddling in bed. Does that sound like a workable approach?

MR. ELLIS: Yeah, it does. It would be so much easier to talk about it outside the scene. It's strange; it never occurs to me to talk about sex or playing until we're actually doing it, and then it feels like it's too late.

DR. ROBBINS: Your wife may even be relieved to have you initiate this conversation, especially when talking about sex is hard for you. A good Dom will often take pride in a sub who can respectfully articulate their need, desires, and limits.

MR. ELLIS: Do you think so?

DR. ROBBINS: Well, I can't be sure, but there is one way to find out; initiate the conversation with her outside of sex time. Perhaps after dinner, or when your children go to sleep, or maybe just go for a walk and bring it up then.

MR. ELLIS: That feels right.

DR. ROBBINS: Good, I'm glad. And remember, you may feel shy or fearful when you broach the subject with your wife, just like you did here today with me. If that happens, trust in the relationship. Have faith that your wife will listen to you in a loving and understanding way.

MR. ELLIS: I'll try.

DR. ROBBINS: And be open to the possibilities. This may lead to more creative scenes with warm-up periods that actually make the whole experience hotter. Maybe you'll both go shopping for floggers of varying weights. Perhaps she'll flog you with your shirt on as a warm up, and then rip it off you in a rush of Dominance and passion. There are many places this can go.

MR. ELLIS: Wow. I never thought of all that. I felt like it was my fault for getting a better body and turning my wife on so much that I just had to bear down and take it.

DR. ROBBINS: And you want to take it, and that's fine. You just need to communicate to your wife how you feel most comfortable taking it. You're entitled to have the great body you've worked for and a sex life that goes at your pace.

MR. ELLIS: This is so helpful. I feel a lot better. Maybe I'll talk to her tonight, after we watch TV, right before we go to bed.

DR. ROBBINS: Sounds like a good plan. You'll let me know what happens next week, okay?

MR. ELLIS: I will. Thanks, Doc. . . . I mean, thanks Michael.

DR. ROBBINS: You're very welcome, Frank, and thank you.

(Mr. Ellis exits.)

Had Frank Ellis known how to find a kink aware professional, what questions to ask, and what red flags to watch out for, he might have had an experience much closer to the version presented in the second vignette. But how would he find these clinicians, what questions should he be asking them, and what indications from the therapist should he be looking for to help ensure the clinician is culturally competent?

FINDING A THERAPIST: THE KINK AWARE PROFESSIONALS DATABASE

As a primary resource for locating kink aware professionals near you, there is none better than the Kink Aware Professionals (KAP) database, hosted by the National Coalition for Sexual Freedom. This database contains contact information, not only for counselors, therapists, and psychologists, but also for accountants, financial advisors, attorneys, wellness practitioners, wedding officiators, private investigators, and more.

Los Angeles–based psychotherapist Guy Baldwin developed this database in 1982. He recognized people's need for referrals to therapists who had a working knowledge of BDSM and Kink, and no prejudice against it. Through Baldwin's media and therapeutic contacts, the list grew over the years to where it was difficult for Baldwin to manage both his successful practice and the growing list. It was in 1994 when San Francisco community activist and writer Race Bannon took over the maintenance of the now-sizable database of kink aware professionals and gave it its now-famous moniker. Over the years, the database continued to grow until, in January 2006, Bannon turned over management of the KAP list to the National Coalition for Sexual Freedom.

> Guy and Race knew that people who enjoy the adventurous side of sex often end up having a difficult time finding mental health professionals sensitive to their needs. Too often clients hear that it's their sexuality that's the problem. That's rarely the case. The usual issues facing these clients aren't related to their sexual interests at all, but the sex-negative bias of some psychotherapists gets in the way of effective therapy. [2]

In addition to the KAP list, make use of your community contacts, networks, friends, and family when choosing a therapist. Oftentimes the most successful referrals are ones made by people you know personally or professionally. As an additional resource, the National Coalition for Sexual Freedom published a paper in 2010 entitled *A Guide to Choosing a Kink Aware Therapist*, by Keely Kolmes, PsyD, and Geri Weitzman, PhD.

FORMS OF ASSISTANCE

Sometimes a therapist isn't what you'll need. Perhaps you're looking for a mentor? A solid book on S/M practice? A class or seminar on bootblacking or whip cracking? Maybe you're looking for something more academic?

There are resources that have been around long enough to have demonstrated both staying power and usefulness.

Community resources are sometimes your best guides and teachers. The classics when it comes to books, organizations, and websites are:

Leather/KINK/Fetish/BDSM Community Organizations

Society of Janus (San Francisco)
The Leathermen's Discussion Group (San Francisco)
The Eulenspiegel Society (New York City)
New England Leather Alliance (Boston)
Black Rose (Washington, DC)
Threshold (Los Angeles)

Leather/Kink/Fetish/BDSM Websites or National Organizations

National Coalition for Sexual Freedom
Leather Leadership Conference
The Kink Academy
The Carter/Johnson Leather Library

Books

The New Bottoming Book, by Dossie Easton and Janet Hardy
The New Topping Book, by Dossie Easton and Janet Hardy
SM 101: A Realistic Introduction, by Jay Wiseman

In terms of an academic approach to Kink and BDSM sexualities, the following resources and organizations are a good place to begin.

Academic Organizations

The Community Academic Consortium for Research on Alternative Sexualities (CARAS)
The Leather Archives and Museum

Academic Books

Sadomasochism: Powerful Pleasures, edited by Peggy J. Kleinplatz, PhD, and Charles Moser, PhD, MD
Safe, Sane, and Consensual: Contemporary Perspectives on Sadomasochism, edited by Darren Langdridge and Meg Barker
Dark Eros: The Imagination of Sadism, by Thomas Moore
Urban Aboriginals, by Geoff Mains

QUESTIONS, RED FLAGS, AND INDICATORS

> At my first session, I told my therapist that I was in a Daddy-boy relationship and the therapist said, "I know what a Daddy-boy relationship means to me, to different BDSM writers, and to other clients of mine, but what does a Daddy-boy relationship mean to you—and how does that dynamic manifest in your relationship?" I knew then that we were a good match. Even though he knew about Daddy-boy relationships, he wanted to know about me and mine.
>
> —Bryan, thirty-three-year-old gay man, leatherboy, kinkster, switch, and graduate student in sociology (Brooklyn, NY)

A therapist is not always going to be the incompetent horror that Frank Ellis encountered in his traumatic consultation. As in Jessie's case, sometimes a therapist, however educated or well-intentioned, just doesn't have the knowledge and experience to do culturally competent work. In other instances, a therapist may go beyond what might be considered basic kink awareness, as in Bryan's case. Remember that you're looking for someone who doesn't automatically pathologize, is sexually open-minded, comfortable with the subject of sex in general, and either knowledgeable of BDSM, Kink, Leather, and Fetish sexualities or willing to educate themselves.

When consulting with a potential therapist, one of the most important questions you can ask is, "What sort of training or education have you had in human sexuality and the range of sexual behaviors?" Knowing that a great majority of counselors and therapists receive little specific training in sexuality, this question—when asked candidly—can sometimes be the only question you'll need to ask. The response will lead, or not lead, to a fruitful dialogue. If you are more comfortable referring to a list of helpful questions, we recommend you consider posing the following:

- Are you familiar with BDSM, Leather, Fetish, and Kink sexualities?
- Are you comfortable with these forms of sexuality?
- What is your understanding of these sexualities?
- Do you think it's wrong, sick, immoral, good, bad, healthy, unhealthy, neutral, or _____?
- Is your practice or agency listed in any Kinky or Alternative Sexuality resources, websites, or guides?
- Are you familiar with any books on the subject? If so, have you read any? What did you think of them?
- What sorts of sexual issues do you feel comfortable and confident addressing in your practice?
- What sorts of sexual issues have you addressed in your practice, and how?
- What do you feel uncomfortable or not confident addressing?
- Do you have any hard limits around discussing sexual material in therapy?

Jack, a kinky heterosexual man from Ottawa told us, "You'd be amazed how no one thought they had any limits around sexual material until I started talking about play piercing."[3]

- How do you think your personal feelings—positive, negative, or neutral—about BDSM, Leather, Kink, or Fetish sexuality would affect your work with me?

Red Flags

I was explaining to my prospective therapist what bondage means to me. He asked! "What Bondage Means to Me." That sounds silly, like a school essay. The therapist didn't really say anything. I was completely open. I always am. It's San Francisco after all. We're lucky here, I guess. Anyhow, when the conversation turned to bondage, he was squirming around in his chair, couldn't make eye contact, and kept crossing and uncrossing his legs. He was either turned on or revolted. I'll never know, 'cause I got up and left. I chose to pretend that I almost made him cum in his pants. I guess it makes me feel powerful, when I was really feeling misunderstood.

—Leanne, a twenty-four-year-old femme, bottom kinkster,
and blogger (San Francisco, CA)

Like Leanne, it's important that you trust your instincts. Whether she was turning him on or making him uncomfortable, it was not a good match. Be conscious of indicators that your prospective therapist may not be right for you. Some red flags to be aware of include body language or talk that might indicate discomfort with the subject(s), knee-jerk reactions based on sexual assumptions, or an overconfidence about dealing with sexual issues that may not hold up to more detailed questioning.

Be mindful of the feeling of being continually led back to the question that there is something inherently wrong about your sexuality, or sex in general. If you're there to talk about vocational anxiety and your therapist keeps bringing the subject back to a problem with your desire to practice suspension bondage, there's a disconnect, to put it mildly. Phrases like "you people" or "people like you," an inability to make eye contact, or a rolling of the eyes are some of the most obvious indications that you should be heading for the door. Other indicators may be subtler. Again, trust your feelings and don't be afraid to ask questions or make personal disclosures to gauge comfort levels.

What to Disclose? How to Disclose?

The first time someone suggested I be this open I was pissed and frustrated. How was I supposed to talk to my therapist about being a Dominant who had secret submissive fantasies about being fisted? When I was coming up as a kid, no one even talked about sex. It just wasn't done. I had to accept the fact that it wasn't 1951 anymore. I'm seventy-five years old and I'd better get comfortable talking about my sex life, because no one was going to do it for me. My healthcare is my responsibility.

—Jackson, seventy-five-year-old Leather Dominant, curious fisting submissive, and film director (Austin, TX)

If we're expected, on an initial job interview, to practice restraint in what we say and how we say it, the converse is true for the initial therapy interview. It's best to let it all hang out. Pretending you're perfect, presenting some skillfully constructed artifice, or pretending you, like a Mattel doll, have no genitals or anus is a waste of your time and money. The time to make disclosures about yourself and your sexuality is in that first initial session. We're not telling you it's easy. Most things worth doing aren't.

But, what do you say? That is up to you and will be guided by your unique erotic experiences and practice, and how important they are to your life and health. Here are some of the examples from the men and women we've spoken with who've approached the topic of their sexuality openly during the first session with a therapist.

KATHERINE: I enjoy BDSM. I'm into submission and body modification. I just want to get it all out there. That's exactly what I would say to a therapist in the very first session. I have no shame, and why should I?

PATRICK: One of the things that has made it hard (makes it hard), for me to seek help with some of the problems in my life is that my sexuality is a bit outside the norm. And often, people jump to conclusions, assuming that my life problems and my sexuality are automatically connected. They might be, but no more so than the sexuality of any other person out there. In our work together, I would need to be confident you wouldn't jump to those conclusions.

SKIP: I had a therapist I saw for a long time say, "I've never really believed in bisexuality. Basically, you're gay or straight. If you end up with a guy or a girl, that's what you are." Then he sort of quizzed me—asked me if I thought about/enjoyed kissing a guy, or thought about guys' penises (he already knew I was married to a woman and enjoyed lots of hetero sex). I then basically had to prove to him that I was bi, by recounting in (luscious) detail an encounter I had with a guy. (He squirmed a bit—the therapist, not the guy. Okay, the guy squirmed too.) But, despite all that, once that was out, he was genuine, and even came back a while later, and told me that he understood how someone could be bisexual and that I had helped him to learn and understand something that was entirely new and against his assumptions.

PAUL: Explaining I'm a Top or bottom, a Dominant or submissive is easy compared with having to tell you I'm into puppy play and dealing with the fear that you might think that means I'm into Bestiality. But, I guess puppy play is a little new on the BDSM scene, so I don't mind explaining to you what it is and what I get out of it.

LETICE: I am with Paul on that one. I know people hear about age play and automatically jump to Pedophilia—which it is *not*—and I'm okay with explaining the difference. It's obscure enough (probably because people have a lot of shame around it) that I would be entirely okay with explaining to my therapist what it is and what it isn't (and what it means to me).

BILLY: I love to get spanked, Mr. Therapist, but I don't expect you to do the spanking. You're off the hook with that one. All you have to do is not blush when I mention it.

WHEN YOU KNOW IT'S RIGHT

I knew the client/therapist match was right for me when the therapist was able to laugh with me. This really didn't happen until the third or fourth session. People tell me that therapists aren't supposed to laugh. Whatever. I'm a comedian and, like many of my ilk, I use my humor to deal with a lifetime of alienation and pain. How could someone understand my pain without the ability to join me in laughing at some of life's absurdities? You can't get my dark side if you can't lighten up and join me on the lighter side of things.

—Lila, fifty-four-year-old comedian, sexual shadow explorer, and self-professed armchair psychologist (Snoqualmie, WA)

Knowing what feels right about a client-therapist match is going to be subjective because everyone's sense of what feels right is going to vary. However, if the therapist appears tuned in to your experience and is in the moment with you—particularly if he or she doesn't know that much about your sexuality—this is a good sign. A willingness to suspend judgment and simply listen is most effective for helping people to feel at ease and to experience the match as a positive one. Like Lila, many people were clear that the ability to laugh was important. There are times to take life and ourselves seriously and times when we can be playful. In relating to a sexual minority that "plays" with sex and often refers to sex and BDSM scenes as "play," it helps to have a therapist who can—on some level—join you in some of the more playful aspects of looking at life and sexuality.

Perhaps Anne, a heterosexual schoolteacher from San Luis Obispo, sums it up best: "Ultimately, the client-therapist relationship, like any other close relationship, needs to feel right. I don't know what that 'feels right' is for everyone. I knew what it was for me. You know it when you feel it and you certainly know it when you don't."

And, to echo Jackson, your healthcare is your responsibility. Don't expect someone to understand you if you refuse to show them who you are.

Chapter Eight

Walking on the Outside

So, what has all this been about? This psychological inquiry into the sexually outside? Let's revisit some of the main themes interwoven throughout *Sexual Outsiders*.

FOR GOOD OR FOR EVIL

Contrary to popular misconceptions that BDSM is either "bad" or "good," it is a neutral force. When applied to a healthy relationship, BDSM can be playful, a growth experience, highly intimate, and gratifying. When applied to an unhealthy relationship, it can be traumatic, destructive, a barrier to intimacy, and toxic.

YOU ARE NOT ALONE . . .

All healthy kink behavior and practices are grounded in, and surrounded by, community. There is a thriving and healthy subculture organized around BDSM in the United States and in many other countries around the world. While this is often an underground community, it has developed clear ethical values, standards, recognized practices that minimize risk, and effective ways of mentoring and educating those new to BDSM.

. . . BUT YOU ARE UNIQUE

There is no one right way of practicing the craft of BDSM. There is no one correct way of being kinky. Though many people adopt BDSM sexuality as an intrinsic part of their identity and construct their lives around it, there are many people who don't, but who are just as kinky. One way is not better or worse than the other, right, or wrong, just different ways of approaching erotic self-expression. There is no single and correct way of building a sexual identity. We need to respect people's autonomy in how they choose to discover and express their sexualities.

POWER IS HOT

BDSM often uses a power differential to create distance and mystery, the structure of which ultimately allows for an intensely connected sexual experience. BDSM is one way to eroticize power.

THE DILEMMA OF SHAME

For sexualities that deviate from what is viewed as normal, or good, shame can be exponential. Because of ignorance, stigma, and squick reactions, people who express BDSM sexuality have to contend with risks related to unhealthy shame. BDSM communities have handled the fallout from unhealthy shame by creating forums, clubs, and institutions to offer peer support, to educate medical and mental health professionals, and to advocate for people's rights.

FACING PREJUDICE AND DISCRIMINATION AS SEXUAL OUTSIDERS

In chapter 7, we described some of the data from the 2008 National Coalition for Sexual Freedom (NCSF) survey of discrimination experienced by members of BDSM communities. Prejudicial attidues have also marked the interactions of kink-identified people with police, judges, doctors, nurses, and employers, as well as family members and friends.

We include here a few reports from that survey, about other areas of stigmatized interaction with social institutions in America:

> "My doctor, even though he was advised of my lifestyle, decided that he would take it upon himself to call the police when I had bruises on me. It took me a long time explaining to the detectives as to why it wasn't domestic violence. My husband was even brought in for questioning."

> "[I experienced a] loss of custody and supervised visitation [was] ordered because I was deemed to be in a 'perverse' sexual lifestyle 'outside of the confines of the social moral norm' . . . no kidding . . . that's what the judge said."

"After being violently assaulted and robbed by a former boyfriend, I went to make a report with the police. When the police questioned the perpetrator, he notified them that I am a professional Dominatrix and am involved in S&M practices. Upon finding out about my involvement with the fetish community, the law enforcement officers dismissed my complaint, explaining that I 'probably liked to get beat up.'"

"My husband was out [as kinky] at his place of work for seven years without repercussions. He had just received a substantial \$4.00-an-hour raise and had always received outstanding performance reviews. When a new facilities manager was hired last year, that all changed. This new manager 'took issue' with our lifestyle, cornered him in private, and told him he was a sick fuck and in serious need of psychiatric counseling. He then proceeded to go on a witch hunt and managed to find a 'semi-legit' reason after several months to have him terminated."

These are just a few examples of the reports collected in that 2008 NCSF survey. The survey had 3,058 respondents, and 37.5 percent of those had experienced some sort of discrimination, harassment, or prejudice. There are some very deep cultural and psychological dynamics that form the foundation for the stigma of BDSM, which we explore next.

THE CASTRATION OF POWER

If we interpret *castration* to mean the removal of power, whether applied to a male, female, or inanimate object, then people, concepts, and movements can be castrated. In a country and society where we, at least in the last century and a half, strive for equality and justice, *power* has become something of a dirty word, the problem child we hide away on family holidays when everything is supposed to be picture perfect, poised, and presentable. Consensual power exchange is erroneously conflated with abuse of authority, exploitation, imbalance, patriarchy, and violence, but like the world of BDSM itself, power exchange is none of these things. Power is energy and, like we said about electricity in chapter 4, it is neutral. It takes on a positive or negative cast depending on how and where it is applied. Consider the words powerful or disempowering. Both are expressions of power—one bestowing and one taking away—depending on the intentions of the entity in control.

Members of BDSM communities turn a deft hand at manipulating and playing with the relinquishing and bestowing of power, and perhaps the playful and sometimes unpredictable movement of power is one of the main characteristics that makes BDSM so upsetting to outside eyes in more mainstream societies.

Our mainstream societies also have a problem with sex. Even when we are able to talk about sex openly as a culture, we want it to stay equal, clean, and (preferably) private. Removing power differences supposedly civilizes sex and makes it more processed and safe for our modern society. This desire for the illusion of equality has inarguably altered the sexual playing field. We have democratized sex. We've made it a polite, clean, and egalitarian exchange. We've watered it down from its primal essence into an often tasteless and colorless experience. Just ask the many men and women in couple's therapy for unsatisfying sex lives, as illustrated in Esther Perel's *Mating in Captivity*.

Our emphasis on equality and egalitarianism leaves little room for spontaneity and fire.

BDSM upsets this apple cart.

The democratization and imposition of egalitarianism on human sexuality have left us with a cultural landscape where we believe that power differences are an impingement or threat to sexual and relational fulfillment. Though we will be the first to state that society is culturally indebted to the women's movement (as we are to the civil rights and GLBT freedom struggles as well) for innumerable contributions to the politics of human sexuality, one result has been the strong impulse to create an erotic playing field that is highly processed and quite democratic in its execution. The problem is that this environment leaves little room for erotic power.

Power differences are inherent in all relationships. Though we have striven, and will continue to strive, to ensure that all people be treated equally under the law, we are not by definition "created" equal. Some of us are more creative; others more intelligent; some of us have more energy, and others are more lethargic; some of us are more adventurous and want to explore, and others are more concerned with building homes and hearths. We inherit disparities of socioeconomic class, race, gender, and education to name just a few. Though these differences should not affect how we are treated under the law, they can and do distinguish us from one another. We are different, and not only is that differentness okay, but it can also be a springboard from which many erotic adventures can begin. Power is an intrinsic part of sexuality. Even from the most heteronormative perspective, there is often the Conqueror (the Penetrator) and the vanquished (the receptive partner), or as we referred to them in chapter 1: the "Initiator" and the "receiver."

There are power differentials in all our relationships, and the denial of this is where the democratization of sex fails us. To ignore these inherent power differences leaves us devoid of a very pleasurable aspect of sexuality. The ability to play with power, manipulate power, and exchange power opens doors to more colorful and exciting parts of our sexual landscape.

SEXUAL FREEDOM IS NOT POLITICALLY CORRECT

Expressions of sexual and erotic freedom may not always agree with what we think freedom and liberty should look like, even from within BDSM communities. We can have conversations about what we like or dislike, and believe is okay or not okay. Sometimes these conversations can obstruct the greater principle that sexual freedom is more important than our own individual likes, dislikes, and opinions.

Just as conversations around edge play have been shut down with a dismissive, "That's gross," so have entire worlds been shut down with the expression, "That's not politically correct."

Sage recounted a story for us that speaks to this very issue.

I was at a big BDSM/Kink retreat weekend in the Southwest. Thursday through Sunday—men and women from all over that part of the country arrived on everything from Harleys to minivans to celebrate together and enjoy the rare experience to be openly kinky outdoors—day and night. It was like Kinkapolooza—a special annual event that people planned their whole year around. There were all kinds of scenes going on—floggings, whippings, energy pulls, nude yoga, white T-shirt water-gun fights, high-protocol service, and play piercing. There was a spiritual circle, labyrinths to walk in meditation, a daily book club, and kink-related recovery meetings. This was a diverse and open-minded band of merrymakers.

Powerplay is tough for people, even for those of us within the community. Displays of real or enacted power differentials sometimes trigger someone, and suddenly there's a problem. One person or persons gets their socially appropriate knickers in a twist and starts to dictate what is "right" or "wrong." This is always dicey and risky business to do when the intention of an entire event is to celebrate all forms of consensual erotic expression.

That said, I treasure spaces like these, even when there's a disagreement. This was one of the biggest and most divisive disagreements I've ever witnessed.

It was Saturday afternoon and the event was in full swing. Everyone had arrived and it was a clear, mild sunny day. Scenes were going on all around—under the sun, by the pool, in the hills, and in the dungeon tents. It was perfect.

I knew of Master CJ and his boy taylor just from being around the scene. They'd been together for years and were great, loving guys. They loved powerplay. One of the ways they enacted their powerplay at this event was for taylor to pull Master CJ around the grounds in a rickshaw-type carriage. taylor would pull while Master CJ reclined above him in the carriage seat holding a buggy whip. Whenever taylor wasn't maintaining the pace his

Master wanted, CJ would flick him across the back and shoulders with the whip. "Hurry up, boy" or "Slow down, boy" we would hear, depending.

Under so-called ordinary circumstances a scene like this wouldn't raise so much as an eyebrow. However, in this instance, it raised some eyebrows and some outcries of protest and disgust.

You see, Master CJ was white and taylor was black.

People got really upset. The racial disparity in this power differential was too much for some of us. It didn't seem to make a difference that CJ and taylor's play was consensual and pleasurable for them both.

Some people were vocally critical, others looked on with disgust, and still others went to some of the organizers complaining that this type of play was inappropriate, politically incorrect, and should be stopped. There was a huge spontaneous discussion that afternoon and I voiced my opinion strongly.

I stated that my feelings about their play were irrelevant. Their ability to play safely and freely, without the judgment of their peers, was more important than any of our feelings on the matter. I had a very strong conviction about this.

People argued that this "type of scene" should be done in the privacy of a cabin or a tent. What about all the other scenes a person may find disturbing, I argued? Do we poll everyone and allow only those scenes that everyone is "okay with" to occur outdoors? I think that's ridiculous!

Plus, how could CJ or taylor get a rickshaw into their cabin or tent?

I understand how race play and racial disparities in powerplay scenes can be disturbing. Racism is baggage we carry around collectively as a country and culture. It's a collective stain on our history. The ways black men and women have been treated from slavery until, in some cases, the present day is reprehensible. That, however, is not what is happening here, now, in the present. What is happening is that two very free and consenting men are playing with power, and, I argued, they have just as much a right to play as we all do. We don't get to determine if someone's kink is right or wrong, no matter how it may offend or trigger us.

Are children or animals involved? That's always my first question. My next question: Is this consensual? Is anyone being hurt? If the answers are no, then carry on. Have fun!

People getting their political or social sensibilities about right and wrong offended does not constitute someone being hurt. If you don't like it, go away. Look elsewhere. This event is happening on eight acres of land! Go somewhere else.

I was relieved when the organizers, though clearly concerned about the high level of emotion around this, supported CJ and taylor's right to play. To have them censored would have felt unjust and totally out of sync with the environment of sexual freedom we had collectively created.

Now perhaps I could understand people trying to stop this kind of a scene if it was being done publicly, say, walking down Main Street in Everywheresville, America, on an average Tuesday, but this was a private, contained area where we had all invested in celebrating our diversity and exercising the freedom of erotic expression. I'm sorry, but your own personal discomforts about race don't give you the right to tell people how and where they should play.

Sexual freedom is more important than our own petty likes and dislikes, even if—in this instance—the opinions of CJ and taylor's critics had a great deal of political, social, and racial force and baggage behind them. Still, to shut down their erotic expression because of the discomfort of one person or a hundred people would have been contrary to the principle of sexual freedom.

> Sexual freedom is not politically correct.

Sage continued, "It's like gay marriage. The issue of marital rights is more important to me than humoring some ignorant person worried about how they're going to explain to their kid that Jack has two mommies. Please! I don't care about your discomfort talking to your damn kid. I'm focused on the larger issue."

WHY SEXUAL FREEDOM?

Sexual freedom is advocating acceptance for a group of people who are seekers, who are often considered outsiders. Though they may be outside exploring dangerous and wild terrain, they can return to their communities with discoveries, experiences, and broader perspectives that can enrich the lives of those who remain at home.

There are many reasons to be a warrior for sexual freedom, a fighter against the war on sex—the innocent natural act of sex is maligned and vilified by social, religious, legal, and educational institutions. The squelching of sexual freedom promotes shame and self-hatred in people suffering with how to be true to who they are. The war on sex and sexual freedom is inherently divisive.

In the words of Marty Klein, therapist, sociologist, and author of *America's War on Sex: The Attack on Law, Lust and Liberty*:

> America's War on Sex is a coordinated attack on anything that makes sexual expression safer, healthier, more comfortable, more pleasurable, more understandable, or more acceptable. That is, anything that makes sexuality a normal part of life. Since most Americans grow up learning that their sexual impulses

are bad, as adults they are vulnerable to mistrusting their neighbors' sexual
impulses. To deal with their anxiety, they attempt to control their neighbors'
sexual expression. This use of public policy to reduce personal anxiety is what
drives the desire to censor others' sexual expression . . . rather than fighting
sexual expression, society should be fighting sexual ignorance and poor sexual
decision-making. [1]

The war on sexual freedom keeps people apart, encourages suspicion, resent-
ment, and jealousy. Fighting for sexual freedom has parallels with every
other social struggle for equality, recognition, and civil liberties, from wom-
en's suffrage to the black freedom struggle to the more recent fights for
transgender and intersex visibility. But, also of prime importance, the fight
for sexual freedom is important because it is a stage on which the hero can
act; it provides an opportunity for Heroism in a general and Jungian sense.

THE OUTSIDER AS HERO

BDSM was a calling for me, a calling in the way some people talk about
religious vocations. It never seemed frightening to me, though my friends,
lover, and family misunderstood it. Through my BDSM journey, and through
seeing how my relationship to my own healthy sexuality has transformed me,
opened me up, and helped me become a fuller and more complete person, they
all came to experience richness and beauty where once they saw only darkness
and danger.

> —Phil, fifty-seven-year-old kink switch and professor (Ann Arbor, MI)

In *The Hero with a Thousand Faces*, Joseph Campbell depicts the recurring
theme in multiple mythological and folk tales of the curious seeker who
leaves home, journeys into unknown realms, and returns from his or her
quests transformed—bearing tales, teachings, and gifts for their communities.

From Prometheus to Theseus to Gautama Sakyamuni to Luke Skywalker,
the sojourner continually sets forth to explore unknown worlds, to claim the
fire, to slay the dragon, to recapture the gold, or to achieve spiritual enlightenment. Venturing alone and very much outside of what would be considered
normal or comfortable, these heroes risk their lives, sanity, and innocence to
gain the wisdom, tools, and power they eventually return home with.

We assert that both the hero and his or her village are of equal importance. How can the village grow and develop without the knowledge gleaned
from the hero's journey, and how could the hero persevere without the support of her loved ones, her home, and her community, if only as a dream to
cling to in moments of trial and pain—that dream of enlightened return.

"The herald or announcer of the adventure, therefore, is often dark, loath-
ly, or terrifying, judged evil by the world; yet if one could follow, the way

would be opened through the walls of day into the dark where the jewels glow."[2] Campbell is saying that the path, the mode, and the call to adventure may be misunderstood or maligned by society, but venturing onto that path, undertaking that adventure, may bring riches, light, and wisdom from something once thought to be evil or bad.

MY SON THE HERO

My son Daniel is my hero, quite literally. When he came out to me as gay, I was a basket case. I'm sad to admit I didn't respond very well. Somehow we worked through it. He already lived so far away and I felt so helpless, so powerless to protect him from all the things I was told being a gay man led to, or was defined by: drug addiction, STDs—especially HIV—alcoholism, promiscuity, prejudice, and violence. I kept remembering what happened to that poor boy Matthew Shepard and all the other assaulted gay men whose traumas never even make the news. I prayed every night that my son would be safe.

He explained to me that being gay wasn't a choice, that he'd known he was gay for as long as he could remember. He just didn't always have a name for it. He said figuring out what being gay meant to him was his journey and all he needed from me was my love and support. He had to figure this out for himself, he said, or he would never be at peace. Instead he'd be living some sort of lie, some horrible half-life. As much as I was afraid of everything bad my dear son might encounter on his path, I knew I had to support him and love him.

So, Daniel began to come out—to his coworkers, friends, and members of our family. Most people embraced him, but some did not. Daniel's journey as a gay man was already teaching me things. Sadly, I learned that some of the people I believed to be loving and opened-minded were not.

Daniel dated, had sex, wrote op-ed pieces for some local papers, spoke at his former high school for an anti-bullying campaign, and went to grad school. He even told me once that he'd dabbled in some kinky stuff. Some of these things are hard for a mother to hear, but it was my job to listen, especially since my husband—Daniel's father—had passed away. I was his only parent. Whether I was comfortable with some of these discussions wasn't as important as my desire to be there for my son when he needed me.

So, Daniel ventured out into the world—a proud, strong gay man with his head held high. I may have worried about him, but I was so proud of the man he'd become. My beautiful little boy had grown up to be a beautiful man, inside and out. There were many years—the early years—where Daniel was promiscuous and drank a little too much. He said, later, that it was "just a part of what I was going through." Meanwhile, I stayed home, knitted, tended the garden, prayed for my son's safety, and attended PFLAG meetings.[3] I was amazed how many young people are ostracized by their families for being gay, bisexual, lesbian, or transgender. Now we have the word *queer* too, I guess. Hard to keep up with it all, huh?

Today Daniel is a professor of social psychology with an emphasis on the evolution of sexual minorities. He's been in books, articles, and on radio and television. He's finishing his first book as I speak. His husband, Brent, is like a son to me, and their children, Casper and Katlyn, are the most precious things in my life—and here I always thought I'd never have grandchildren.

The point is Daniel is a hero. He ventured out into the unknown to discover deeper truths about himself and the world. He changed and grew, underwent challenges, setbacks, and great successes. Even so, he felt the need to give back, to bring something back to others. He made a career out of it. He also came back home to me, metaphorically, and through his journey I grew. He gave me so much, taught me, and opened my world. Through his courage, I have a better life, a more open mind, and a beautiful family. Daniel changed the world, even if in a small way. He changed his world on a grand scale and he changed mine forever.

That's what makes a hero.

—Marilyn, sixty-three-year-old retired toymaker, artist,
and proud mother of Daniel

Heroes like Daniel, Darren, Alicia, Phil, and Michael walk various paths and wear armor we may be unaccustomed to, but their journeys and the wisdom they glean teach us valuable lessons, if we choose to listen. Four of those lessons are:

• Power is complex and dynamic, and we are always contending with being both powerful and powerless at the same time.
• It is important to healing and growth to embrace the Shadow and to integrate one's experiences into a fuller, more realistic image of ourselves as persons.
• It is vital to our health and well-being that we play, including sexually.
• Contending with shame, prejudice, and discrimination calls for action from all of us, collectively and individually.

As long as there are social constructs creating and enforcing the stark polarities between better and worse, light and dark, depraved and revered, Madonna and whore, there will always be transgressive ideas, tantalizing fears, and thrilling fantasies hiding in the shadows, and, as long as light continues to cast shadows, there will always be those who choose, or who are forced, to walk on the fringes.

There will always be children who color outside the lines, proclaiming with innocent pride, "Isn't my drawing special too?"

Exploring the unknown, or simply giving it respect with a suspension of judgment, is an important step toward health and integration—for the outsiders across the world, for our society, and for those silent, secret outsiders living deep within us all.

Notes

INTRODUCTION

1. Regarding the words *community* and *communities*, which the authors use throughout the book, we recognize that the word *community*, when applied to the world of BDSM, refers to an often overlapping series of communities.

2. *Polyamory* is a relationship paradigm incorporating more than one intimate relationship at a time with the knowledge and consent of everyone involved. It is often referred to by its abbreviation: *poly*.

3. Glenn Wilson, "Personality, Sexual Behaviour and Marital Satisfaction," in *Hans Eysenck: Consensus and Controversy*, ed. Sohan Modgil and Celia Modgil, 263–86 (London: Falmer Press, 1986).

4. K. L. Guadalupe and D. Lum, *Multidimensional Contextual Practice: Diversity and Transcendence* (Belmont, CA: Thomson Brooks/Cole, 2005).

5. *Squick* is the emotional gut reaction to stimuli that one finds repulsive or disgusting—a combination of *squirm* and *ick*. It is meant to point our attention to the visceral reaction, without implying a moral condemnation or judgment. The term comes from the BDSM community.

6. Outside of the United States, most mental health professionals use the ICD—the International Classification of Diseases manual, maintained by the World Health Organization. The DSM and the ICD both have fetishism and sadomasochism, in some form, on their lists of sexual disorders.

7. Though popularly quoted, there is no evidence that Sigmund Freud actually said this.

8. R. Eher, C. Grunehut, S. Fruehwald, P. Frottier, B. Hobl, and M. Aigner, "A Comparison between Exclusively Male Target and Female/Both Sexes Target Child Molesters on Psychometric Variables, Dsm-Iv Diagnoses and Mtc:Cm3 Typology," in *Sex Offender Treatment: Accomplishments, Challenges, and Future Directions*, ed. M. Miner and E. Coleman, 89–102 (New York: Haworth Press, 2001).

9. W. L. Marshall, "Diagnostic Issues, Multiple Paraphilias, and Comorbid Disorders in Sexual Offenders: Their Incidence and Treatment," *Aggression and Violent Behavior* 12 (2007): 16–35.

10. Susan Wright, *Survey of Discrimination and Violence against Sexual Minorities*, ed. National Coalition for Sexual Freedom, technical report (Baltimore, MD: National Coalition for Sexual Freedom, 2008).

11. E. H. Erikson, *Identity: Youth and Crisis* (New York: Norton, 1968).

1. THE POWER OF LANGUAGE

1. *Fetish*—a sexual attraction to objects, body parts, or situations not conventionally viewed as being sexual in nature.

2. Leopold von Sacher-Masoch, *Venus in Furs* (New York: Penguin, [1870] 2000).

3. This type of erotic play in no way involves nonhuman animals or is in any way related to Bestiality.

4. R. V. Bienvenu II, "The Development of Sadomasochism as a Cultural Style in the Twentieth-Century United States" (PhD diss., Indiana University, 1998).

5. Recon is "the world's largest hook-up site for men into fetish gear." www.recon.com, accessed April 10, 2012.

2. THE CURIOUS NOVICE

1. "FetLife is a FREE Social Network for the BDSM & fetish community. Similar to Facebook and MySpace but run by kinksters like you and me. We think it is more fun that way. Don't you?" www.fetlife.com, accessed April 2012.

2. *Queer* is an umbrella term for sexual minorities that are not heterosexual or do not identify with traditional gender categories of male and female.

3. The Society of Janus (SOJ) is a San Francisco–based support and education organization for people interested in learning about BDSM. "Janus is a pansexual organization; we are open to persons of all genders, sexual orientations (straight/gay/bisexual/etc.) and roles (Top/Dom/switch/bottom/slave/etc.). Janus was founded in August, 1974 by the late Cynthia Slater and Larry Olsen. It is the second-oldest BDSM group in the United States—The Eulenspiegel Society in New York City (founded in 1971), being the oldest." www.soj.org, accessed April 2012.

4. Bondage-A-Go-Go is a fetish-themed dance party that has been held in the city since 1993—making it the longest-running weekly dance event in San Francisco. www.bondage-a-go-go.com, accessed April 2012.

5. The SF Citadel is widely recognized as the Bay Area's premiere Community Dungeon Play Space.

6. Alfred C. Kinsey, Wardell B. Pomeroy, Clyde E. Martin, and Paul H. Gebhard, *Sexual Behavior in the Human Female* (Oxford: Saunders, 1953); W. B. Arndt, J. C. Foehl, and F. E. Good, "Specific Sexual Fantasy Themes: A Multidimensional Study," *Journal of Personality and Social Psychology* 48, no. 2 (1985): 472–80.

7. W. H. Masters, V. E. Johnson, and R. C. Kolodny, *Human Sexuality* (New York: HarperCollins, 1995); J. Richters, R. de Visser, C. Rissel, A. Grulich, A. M. A. Smith, "Demographic and Psychosocial Features of Participants in Bondage and Discipline, 'Sadomasochism' or Dominance and Submission (BDSM): Data From a National Survey," *Journal of Sexual Medicine* 5 (2008): 1660–68.

8. J. Richters, A. E. Grulich, R. O. de Visser, A. M. Smith, and C. E. Rissel, "Sex in Australia: Autoerotic, Esoteric and Other Sexual Practices Engaged in by a Representative Sample of Adults," *Aust N Z J Public Health* 27, no. 2 (2003): 180–90.

9. Black Rose is a BDSM organization based in Washington, DC. It was founded in June of 1987.

10. Gayle S. Rubin, *Deviations: A Gayle Rubin Reader* (Durham, NC: Duke University Press, 2011). The Eulenspiegel Society (TES) is the oldest and largest BDSM support and education group in the United States. TES was founded by Pat Bond and a group of masochists in New York City in 1971.

11. R. V. Bienvenu II, "The Development of Sadomasochism as a Cultural Style in the Twentieth-Century United States" (PhD diss., Indiana University, 1998).

12. Kathy Sisson, "The Cultural Formation of S/M: History and Analysis," in *Safe, Sane and Consensual: Contemporary Perspectives on Sadomasochism*, ed. Darren Langdridge and Meg Barker, 10–34 (New York: Palgrave MacMillan, 2007).

13. The Gay Male S/M Activists (GMSMA), an educational, political, and social group, was founded in 1981 in New York City.

14. The CARAS is "dedicated to the support and promotion of excellence in the study of alternative sexualities, and the dissemination of research results to the alternative sexuality communities, the public, and the research community." https://carasresearch.org, accessed April 2012. Richard Sprott is executive director of the nonprofit organization, which was founded by Richard Sprott, Robert Bienvenu, and David Ortmann in 2005.

3. COMING OUT

1. Though some of the men and women contributing to *Sexual Outsiders* may use the word *vanilla* to describe nonkinky sex, the authors prefer to use the term *traditional* or *classic* when writing in their own voices.

2. B. Link and J. Phelan, "Conceptualizing Stigma," *Annual Review of Sociology* 27 (2001): 363–85. doi: 10.1146/annurev.soc.27.1.363.

4. STORIES OF PERSONAL GROWTH AND HEALING

1. Dossie Easton, "Shadowplay: S/M Journeys to Our Selves," in *Safe, Sane and Consensual: Contemporary Perspectives on Sadomasochism*, ed. Darren Langdridge and Meg Barker, 217–28 (New York: Palgrave Macmillan, 2007), 225.

2. C. G. Jung, *Aion: Researches into the Phenomenology of the Self* (Princeton, NJ: Princeton University Press, [1959] 1978).

3. J. Whitlock, A. Purington, and M. Gershkovich, "Media, the Internet, and Nonsuicidal Self-Injury," in *Understanding Nonsuicidal Self-Injury: Origins, Assessment and Treatment*, ed. Matthew K. Nock, 139–55 (Washington, DC: American Psychological Association, 2009).

4. Kim L. Gratz, "Risk Factors for Deliberate Self-Harm among Female College Students: The Role and Interaction of Childhood Maltreatment, Emotional Inexpressivity, and Affect Intensit/Reactivity," *American Journal of Orthopsychiatry* 76, no. 2 (2006): 238–50. doi:10.1037/0002-9432.76.2.238.

5. WHEN THINGS GO WRONG

1. C. Moser, "BDSM: Psychopathology vs. Healthy Sexual Variant," paper presented at the Society for the Study of Social Problems, April 2009.

2. Kathryn Akemi Ando, "Attitudes and Behaviors Concerning Erotic Breath Control," The Institute for Advanced Study of Human Sexuality, 2009.

3. Dacher Keltner, Deborah Gruenfeld, and Cameron Anderson, "Power, Approach and Inhibition," *Psychological Review* 110, no. 2 (2003): 265–84.

4. Alan Downs, *The Velvet Rage: Overcoming the Pain of Growing Up Gay in a Straight Man's World* (Cambridge, MA: Da Capo Press, 2005).

6. POWER IS HOT

1. Pamela Connolly, "Psychological Functioning of Bondage/Domination/Sado-Masochism (BDSM) Practitioners," *Journal of Psychology and Human Sexuality* 18, no. 1 (2006): 79–120; P. A. Cross and K. Matheson, "Understanding Sadomasochism: An Empirical Examination of Four Perspectives," *J Homosex* 50, nos. 2–3 (2006): 133–66; R. Stoller, *Pain and Passion: A Psychoanalyst Explores the World of S&M* (New York: Plenum Press, 1991).

2. C. Moser and Peggy J. Kleinplatz, eds., *Sadomasochism: Powerful Pleasures* (New York: Harrington Park Press, 2006).

3. The proposed criteria for paraphilias in the DSM-V revision due to be released in 2013 codify this distinction already—the proposal recognizes that having a Paraphilia is not the same as having a mental disorder, so there is now the distinction between a Paraphilia and a paraphilic disorder.

4. G. C. Gonzaga, Dacher Keltner, and D. Ward, "Power in Mixed-Sex Stranger Interactions," *Cognition and Emotion* 22, no. 8 (2008): 1555–68; Dacher Keltner, Deborah Gruenfeld, and Cameron Anderson, "Power, Approach and Inhibition," *Psychological Review* 110, no. 2 (2003): 265–84.

5. C. Moser and E. E. Levitt, "An Exploratory-Descriptive Study of a Sadomasochistically Oriented Sample," *Journal of Sex Research* 23 (1987): 322–37.

6. N. Breslow, L. Evans, and J. Langley, "Comparisons among Heterosexual, Bisexual and Homosexual Male Sado-Masochists," *Journal of Homosexuality* 13, no. 1 (1986): 83–107.

7. J. Rehor, "The Occurrence of Unconventional Sexual Behaviors in Women," San Francisco State University, 2011.

8. H. Brownstein, *The Social Reality of Violence and Violent Crime* (Boston, MA: Allyn & Bacon, 2000); R. Gelles, "Family Violence," *Annual Review of Sociology* 11 (1985): 347–67.

9. N. Scheper-Hughes, "A Talent for Life: Reflections on Human Vulnerability and Resilience," *Ethnos: Journal of Anthropology* 73, no. 1 (2008): 25–56.

10. *Virago*—denotes a woman who is heroic, assertive and agressive, physically strong, and often transgressing traditional feminine roles and styles. A popular contemporary image is the character Ripley in the Alien movies or Katniss Everdeen in the Hunger Games books and movies

11. The DSM-IV defines *Pedophilia* as a psychological disorder when the object of these sexual fantasies, urges, or behaviors is "generally 13 years or younger." Phoenix and Foster were, respectively, sixteen and fourteen when their films were released and, respectively, (approximately) fifteen and thirteen when they were filmed. This information is gathered from the Internet Movie Database and both artists' birthdays.

7. GETTING ASSISTANCE

1. The National Coalition for Sexual Freedom (NCSF) was formed in 1997 by a small group led by Susan Wright under the auspices of the New York SM Activists. The goal was to fight for sexual freedom and privacy rights for all adults who engage in safe, sane, and consensual behavior. Today, the NCSF "is committed to creating a political, legal, and social environment in the United States that advances equal rights for consenting adults who engage in alternative sexual and relationship expressions. The NCSF aims to advance the rights of, and advocate for, consenting adults in the BDSM, Leather, Fetish, Swing, and Polyamory communities through direct services, education, advocacy, and outreach, in conjunction with our partners, to directly benefit these communities." www.ncsfreedom.org, accessed April 2012.

2. National Coalition for Sexual Freedom, "A Brief History of the Kink Aware Professionals Directory," https://ncsfreedom.org/key-programs/kink-aware-professionals/a-brief-history-of-kap.html, accessed April 14, 2012.

3. *Play piercing* is a scene or activity where the skin is pierced with needles, usually, in a temporary way. The term can also refer to the creation of permanent piercings to wear body jewelry, where the initial piercing to attach the jewelry is part of a BDSM scene.

8. WALKING ON THE OUTSIDE

1. M. Klein, personal communication, April 9, 2012.
2. J. Campbell, *The Hero with a Thousand Faces*, 2nd ed. (Princeton, NJ: Princeton University Press, 1973), 53.
3. Parents, Families and Friends of Lesbians and Gays (PFLAG) is "a national support, education and advocacy organization for lesbian, gay, bisexual and transgender (LGBT) people, their families, friends and allies. With 200,000 members and supporters, and local affiliates in more than 350 communities across the United States and abroad, PFLAG is the largest grassroots-based family organization of its kind. PFLAG is a nonprofit organization and is not affiliated with any religious or political institutions." www.pflag.org, accessed April 2012.

Bibliography

Ando, Kathryn Akemi. "Attitudes and Behaviors Concerning Erotic Breath Control." The Institute for Advanced Study of Human Sexuality, 2009.

Arndt, W. B., J. C. Foehl, and F. E. Good. "Specific Sexual Fantasy Themes: A Multidimensional Study." *Journal of Personality and Social Psychology* 48, no. 2 (1985): 472–80.

Bienvenu, R. V., II. "The Development of Sadomasochism as a Cultural Style in the Twentieth-Century United States." PhD dissertation, Indiana University, 1998.

Breslow, N., L. Evans, and J. Langley. "Comparisons among Heterosexual, Bisexual and Homosexual Male Sado-Masochists." *Journal of Homosexuality* 13, no. 1 (1986): 83–107.

Brownstein, H. *The Social Reality of Violence and Violent Crime*. Boston, MA: Allyn & Bacon, 2000.

Campbell, J. *The Hero with a Thousand Faces*. 2nd ed. Princeton, NJ: Princeton University Press, 1973.

Connolly, Pamela. "Psychological Functioning of Bondage/Domination/Sado-Masochism (BDSM) Practitioners." *Journal of Psychology and Human Sexuality* 18, no. 1 (2006): 79–120.

Cross, P. A., and K. Matheson. "Understanding Sadomasochism: An Empirical Examination of Four Perspectives." *J Homosex* 50, nos. 2–3 (2006): 133–66.

Downs, Alan. *The Velvet Rage: Overcoming the Pain of Growing Up Gay in a Straight Man's World*. Cambridge, MA: Da Capo Press, 2005.

Easton, Dossie. "Shadowplay: S/M Journeys to Our Selves." In *Safe, Sane and Consensual: Contemporary Perspectives on Sadomasochism*, edited by Darren Langdridge and Meg Barker, 217–28. New York: Palgrave Macmillan, 2007.

Eher, R., C. Grunehut, S. Fruehwald, P. Frottier, B. Hobl, and M. Aigner. "A Comparison between Exclusively Male Target and Female/Both Sexes Target Child Molesters on Psychometric Variables, DSM-IV Diagnoses and Mtc:Cm3 Typology." In *Sex Offender Treatment: Accomplishments, Challenges, and Future Directions*, edited by M. Miner and E. Coleman, 89–102. New York: Haworth Press, 2001.

Erikson, E. H. *Identity: Youth and Crisis*. New York: Norton, 1968.

Gelles, R. "Family Violence." *Annual Review of Sociology* 11 (1985): 347–67.

Gonzaga, G. C., Dacher Keltner, and D. Ward. "Power in Mixed-Sex Stranger Interactions." *Cognition and Emotion* 22, no. 8 (2008): 1555–68.

Gratz, Kim L. "Risk Factors for Deliberate Self-Harm among Female College Students: The Role and Interaction of Childhood Maltreatment, Emotional Inexpressivity, and Affect Intensit/Reactivity." *American Journal of Orthopsychiatry* 76, no. 2 (2006): 238–50.

Guadalupe, K. L., and D. Lum. *Multidimensional Contextual Practice: Diversity and Transcendence*. Belmont, CA: Thomson Brooks/Cole, 2005.

Jung, C. G. *Aion: Researches into the Phenomenology of the Self.* Princeton, NJ: Princeton University Press, [1959] 1978.

Keltner, Dacher, Deborah Gruenfeld, and Cameron Anderson. "Power, Approach and Inhibition." *Psychological Review* 110, no. 2 (2003): 265–84.

Kinsey, Alfred C., Wardell B. Pomeroy, Clyde E. Martin, and Paul H. Gebhard. *Sexual Behavior in the Human Female.* Oxford: Saunders, 1953.

Link, B., and J. Phelan. "Conceptualizing Stigma." *Annual Review of Sociology* 27 (2001): 363–85.

Mains, Geoff. *Urban Aboriginals: A Celebration of Leathersexuality.* San Francisco: Gay Sunshine Press, 1984.

Marshall, W. L. "Diagnostic Issues, Multiple Paraphilias, and Comorbid Disorders in Sexual Offenders: Their Incidence and Treatment." *Aggression and Violent Behavior* 12 (2007): 16–35.

Masters, W. H., V. E. Johnson, and R. C. Kolodny. *Human Sexuality.* New York: HarperCollins, 1995.

Moore, Thomas. *Dark Eros: The Imagination of Sadism.* Woodstock, CT: Spring Publications, 1990.

Moser, C. "BDSM: Psychopathology vs. Healthy Sexual Variant." Paper presented at the Society for the Study of Social Problems, April 2009.

Moser, C., and E. E. Levitt. "An Exploratory-Descriptive Study of a Sadomasochistically Oriented Sample." *Journal of Sex Research* 23 (1987): 322–37.

Moser, C., and Peggy J. Kleinplatz, eds. *Sadomasochism: Powerful Pleasures.* New York: Harrington Park Press, 2006.

National Coalition for Sexual Freedom. "A Brief History of the Kink Aware Professionals Directory." https://ncsfreedom.org/key-programs/kink-aware-professionals/a-brief-history-of-kap.html. Accessed April 14, 2012.

Perel, Esther. *Mating in Captivity.* New York: Harper, 2007.

Rehor, J. "The Occurrence of Unconventional Sexual Behaviors in Women." San Francisco State University, 2011.

Richters, J., A. E. Grulich, R. O. de Visser, A. M. Smith, and C. E. Rissel. "Sex in Australia: Autoerotic, Esoteric and Other Sexual Practices Engaged in by a Representative Sample of Adults." *Aust N Z J Public Health* 27, no. 2 (2003): 180–90.

Richters, J., R. de Visser, C. Rissel, A. Grulich, and A. M. A. Smith. "Demographic and Psychosocial Features of Participants in Bondage and Discipline, 'Sadomasochism' or Dominance and Submission (BDSM): Data From a National Survey." *Journal of Sexual Medicine* 5 (2008): 1660–68.

Rubin, Gayle S. *Deviations: A Gayle Rubin Reader.* Durham, NC: Duke University Press, 2011.

Sacher-Masoch, L. v. *Venus in Furs.* New York: Penguin, [1870] 2000.

Scheper-Hughes, N. "A Talent for Life: Reflections on Human Vulnerability and Resilience." *Ethnos: Journal of Anthropology* 73, no. 1 (2008): 25–56.

Sisson, Kathy. "The Cultural Formation of S/M: History and Analysis." In *Safe, Sane and Consensual: Contemporary Perspectives on Sadomasochism*, edited by Darren Langdridge and Meg Barker, 10–34. New York: Palgrave MacMillan, 2007.

Stoller, R. *Pain and Passion: A Psychoanalyst Explores the World of S&M.* New York: Plenum Press, 1991.

Whitlock, J., A. Purington, and M. Gershkovich. "Media, the Internet, and Nonsuicidal Self-Injury." In *Understanding Nonsuicidal Self-Injury: Origins, Assessment and Treatment*, edited by Matthew K. Nock, 139–55. Washington, DC: American Psychological Association, 2009.

Wilson, Glenn. "Personality, Sexual Behaviour and Marital Satisfaction." In *Hans Eysenck: Consensus and Controversy*, edited by Sohan Modgil and Celia Modgil, 263–86. London: Falmer Press, 1986.

Wiseman, Jay. *SM 101: A Realistic Introduction.* San Francisco, CA: Greenery Press, 1996.

Wright, Susan. *Survey of Discrimination and Violence against Sexual Minorities.* Edited by National Coalition for Sexual Freedom. Technical Report. Baltimore, MD: National Coalition for Sexual Freedom, 2008.

Index

abandonment, 51, 58, 65; interdependence and, 33
abnormal, normal and, 4
abuse, 13, 74–76; consent and, 147; in teacher-student roleplaying, 112
accidents, 77; with bondage, 79–80; with drugs and alcohol, 78–79; lessons learned from, 80–81
acquiescence, 75
addictions, 12, 153; anger and, 77
aftercare, 38–39, 62, 63; consent and, 76; powerlessness and, 86
age play, 107–116; binary culture and, 116; masturbation and, 104, 115; Pedophilia and, 116, 142; survey results on, 88
aggression, 72, 93; coming out and, 46; impact play and, 97–98; power and, 87
alcohol, 78–79
alexithymia, 67
America's War on Sex: The Attack on Law, Lust and Liberty (Klein), 151
anger, 6, 76–77; with Devon and Pat, 72, 73; power and, 76; shame and, 76, 77
anthropology, 5
Antisocial Personality Disorder, 5
anxiety, 2; personal growth and healing and, 51–65; of therapy refugees, 8
assistance, 119–143; with BDSM and Therapy Project, 123–136; with education, 37–38, 121–123; forms of, 137–138; with KAP, 137; for personal

growth and healing, 119; red flags with, 140; rightness of, 142–143; what and how to disclose, 140–142
As You Like It (Shakespeare), 93
authenticity, 33; stigma and, 46
autoerotic asphyxia, 75; deaths from, 74
autonomy, 33

Baldwin, Guy, 137
balloons, fetishism for, 88
Bardot, Brigitte, 86
Barker, Meg, 60, 138
Batman and Robin, 42
B/D. *See* Bondage and Discipline
BDSM and Therapy Project, 123–136
beatings: consent with, 26; of novice, 25–26
Bestiality, 114–115, 156n2
betrayal, 66
Bienvenu, Robert, 35–36
binary culture, 3–4; age play and, 116; gender identity and, 3
biting, 34
Black Rose, 35, 37, 138
blame, 45
bondage: accidents with, 79–80; definition of, 15; by Devon and Pat, 71; exploration of, 71; fantasy of, 42; masturbation and, 42–43; restraints in, 15; safety with, 36
Bondage-a-Go-Go, 29, 31, 156n4

About the Authors

David M. Ortmann, LCSW, is a psychotherapist, sex therapist, and author in private practice. His work has been published in journals, magazines, and anthologies of fiction and nonfiction. His areas of clinical focus and study are the sexuality of the BDSM, Leather and Kink communities, concepts and theories of masculinity, and the processes of human attachment and differentiation. He speaks locally and nationally in an effort to promote Leather, Kink, and BDSM community visibility and improve clinical psychotherapeutic interventions for these populations.

Ortmann is a member of the National Coalition for Sexual Freedom (NCSF), the American Association of Sexuality Educators, Counselors, and Therapists (AASECT), the Northern California Society for Psychoanalytic Psychology (NCSPP), and is one of the founding members of the Community-Academic Consortium for Research on Alternative Sexualities (CARAS).

Richard A. Sprott, PhD, is a research psychologist in developmental science and lecturer in the Department of Human Development and Women's Studies at California State University, East Bay. He is the executive director of the Community-Academic Consortium for Research on Alternative Sexualities (CARAS), a community-academic partnership to enhance and encourage scientific investigation and scholarly analysis of understudied sexualities, like BDSM and polyamory. He has published in several academic journals and presented papers at community and academic conferences nationwide.